The House and Senate Explained

D0094078

The House

AND

Senate

EXPLAINED

The People's Guide to Congress

ELLEN GREENBERG

W. W. NORTON & COMPANY

New York   London

To Bookie Fisher, who always said it would happen

The text of this book is composed in Bembo
with the display set in Snell Roundhand
Composition by PennSet, Inc.
Manufacturing by Quebecor Printing Book Group.
Book design by Susan Hood

Library of Congress Cataloging-in-Publication Data
Greenberg, Ellen.
  The House and Senate explained : the people's guide to
Congress / Ellen Greenberg ; foreword by Robert MacNeil.
    p.   cm.
  Rev. ed. of: The House & Senate explained. c1986.
  Includes index.
  ISBN 0-393-03984-6.—ISBN 0-393-31496-0 (pbk.)
  1. United States. Congress.—Dictionaries.   2. United
States. Congress.—Handbooks, manuals, etc.
I. Greenberg, Ellen. House & Senate explained.   II. Title.
JK1067.G74   1996
328.73'003—dc20   96-12291
                                                                  CIP

W. W. Norton & Company, Inc., 500 Fifth Avenue,
New York, N.Y. 10110   http://web.wwnorton.com

W. W. Norton & Company Ltd., 10 Coptic Street,
London WC1A 1PU

3   4   5   6   7   8   9   0

Contents

Foreword

by Robert MacNeil

Apathy, anger, disgust, indifference: From the nightly ridicule of David Letterman and Jay Leno, to the furious bombast of talk radio, to the caustic or sardonic tone of much journalism, there is plenty of evidence that Americans are disgusted and disillusioned with the Congress. Besides weak voter turnout and calls for term limits, polls show low rankings for congresspersons among admired professions, resentment of their pay levels and perks, anger at their perceived remoteness from the concerns of ordinary people, disgust with negative campaigning and the sources of money to fuel it, suspicion of favors for special interests, weariness with empty partisanship, and dismay at political gridlock—in general a mood of sourness and disenchantment. Seeing all this, foreigners might think the people in the world's greatest democracy were so alienated from its principal institutions that they'd want to throw out the whole damned system.

Yet if you check the audiences for C-SPAN, and certain programs of CNN and PBS, it is equally obvious that millions of Americans take the Congress very seriously and are greedy for serious coverage of its doings. In particular C-SPAN, the brilliant stepchild of Congress and the cable TV industry, has revealed an amazing appetite for unmediated, unfiltered access to the most routine activities of House and Senate, in all their numbing minutiae—the stuff journalism usually disdains, except to ridicule.

It is easy to ridicule these C-SPAN junkies, until you consider that what addicts them is the actual workings of the democracy we so love to crow over. I think it is a magnificent obsession, and this is the handbook they deserve. It is guidebook, dictionary, and encyclopedia distilled to a usable size. It may not make heroes of congresspersons, but if it helps people understand what they actually do every day, it might even gain them a little respect.

Introduction

The relationship between you, the citizen, and your elected officials is at the heart of our representative form of government. Article I of the Constitution says, "The House of Representatives shall be composed of Members chosen every second year by the People of the several States. . . ." For the Senate, the Seventeenth Amendment ordered the direct election of senators (up to 1913 they were selected by the state legislatures). What it all boils down to is that your elected officials have a duty to represent *you* and a duty to respond to your demands.

Even if you're under voting age (eighteen), you can have your say. The Fourteenth Amendment to the Constitution says: "All persons born or naturalized in the United States, and subject to the jurisdiction thereof, are citizens of the United States and of the State wherein they reside." Your members of Congress represent all the citizens in their district and state; the Constitution says that, too.★

★ The pronoun "he" is used throughout this book, not because Congress contains only he's but because "he/she" and "he and she" are awkward and an impediment to reading.

Do your elected officials represent your views? Not always. For example, other people whom they also represent may have other views, or what you're asking for may go against what they believe is best for the country, or they may simply be pandering to bigger interests. Whatever the reason, one thing is certain: You can't get your agenda seen to if your representative and senators don't know what it is you want done. You have to get in touch and let them know what you're after and why they should pursue the matter. And in order to do that, it's a darn good idea to learn how the system works. That's where this book comes in.

Let me back up for a minute. The coming of cable TV brought us C-SPAN, the Cable Satellite Public Affairs Network. And C-SPAN allowed me to take a good look at what was going on in the House and Senate. I found it fascinating but, because of my ignorance of the process, sometimes boring and many times confusing. I set out on a quest for answers to my questions—what was that sticklike thing, and why was it always being moved around the House of Representatives? Who were those people shuffling papers in front of the Senate?—and a book was born.

A good portion of *The House and Senate Explained: The People's Guide to Congress* is designed to be used first as a dictionary—when you see someone or something and you don't know who he is or what it is; when you hear a word or phrase and don't know what it means. Second, the book is meant to be your guide to the processes of the House of Representatives and the Senate, to help you understand how things get done or not done. Third, the book tells you some of the ways you can become part of the process.

The first section, "The Stage and the Players," explains just what it is you're seeing on your TV screen or from a chamber's gallery. It gives a brief description of the men and women who sit near and on the Speaker's rostrum in the House and the presiding officer's desk in the Senate.

The second section, "The Script: The Words You Hear and What They Mean," is the heart of the book. If you've always thought the word "markup" has to do with what a shopkeeper charges for a product, or that a "memorial" is a way of keeping memory alive, or that a "clean bill" means a bird with a shiny beak, this section will set you straight.

The rules under which the House and Senate operate sometimes differ significantly. When this is the case, a definition is followed by paragraphs headed "In the House" and "In the Senate" explaining each chamber's way of doing things.

Like the section before it, the third section, "Some Frequently Heard Phrases," is meant to help you understand what it *really* is that a member is saying. On the House side the material is arranged so that you can follow a bill's progress straight through to its final passage. Key phrases and dialogue from the more informal Senate are given separate but equal treatment.

The fourth section, "The Legislative Day," is meant as a guide to the *usual* order of each chamber's business. The House day also includes the usual daily meeting times and lists the days set aside for special purposes. If today were Wednesday, the reading clerk might be calling the roll of committees, but if it were the fourth Monday of the month, the House would probably be taking up the business of the District of Columbia.

"The Rocky Road to Passage: How a Bill Becomes a Law" tracks a piece of legislation—one that originates in the House—from its introduction to its final passage.

The next section is all about reaching out, getting in

touch with your senators and representative and letting them know how you feel. It explains how you can find out who represents you and how they can be contacted. It describes how you can see them in action and how you can become part of that action.

The final section gives you a brief rundown of the material available on the Internet. It brings the wizards of yesterday, the people who created our government, face-to-face with the wizards of today.

Most of Congress's work is done in committees. That's where the Appendix comes in. It's a listing of the committees and their subcommittees. If you want to discuss air pollution with a senator or the welfare of miners with a representative, the Appendix will help you uncover which committee or committees have responsibility for what. By the way, the Senate Committee on Environment and Public Works and the House Committee on Economic and Educational Opportunities are the places to go if you're interested in the subject matter of the two examples above.

You may not always deserve what you get, but you don't have to take it lying down. If you think politicians have all the power, ask yourself where that power comes from. The answer is: It comes from you, from me, from us. We have the last word; we have the vote.

Complaining to your next-door neighbor won't get it done. Casting your ballot and then letting your elected officials know how you feel by reaching out will. Don't be a political couch potato. Get up and give 'em hell—or a pat on the head for a job well done—but don't just lie there.

This book could not have been written without Mart, who picked up the slack; or published without Bob

Markel, who found it a home. Thanks, too, to Amy Cherry for asking good questions, to Meredith Fine for fine tuning, and to InnoNet, an innovative nonprofit organization with superior research skill and esprit de corps.

The House and Senate Explained

1

The Stage and the Players

The House

THE STAGE—the Places and
Things You See
See diagrams pages 4 and 5.

a. Mace: Forty-six inches tall, this ancient symbol of legislative authority is in the charge of the sergeant at arms. It's made up of a bundle of thirteen ebony rods tied with silver thongs and ending with a globe topped by a silver eagle with outstretched wings. When the day's session begins, an assistant to the sergeant at arms takes the mace from its cabinet and sets it on a green marble pedestal at the right of the Speaker's desk. When the House is meeting as a committee (see Committee of the Whole, p. 34), the mace is moved to a low white marble pedestal farther to the right. On rare occasions the sergeant at arms may hold the mace in

THE HOUSE OF REPRESENTATIVES: LOOK TOWARD THE SPEAKER'S ROSTRUM

The Stage		*The Players*	
a	Mace	**1**	Sergeant at Arms
b	Speaker's Rostrum	**2**	Speaker's Page
c	Clerk's Lectern	**3 & 4**	Documentarian Pages
d	Hopper	**5**	Parliamentarian
e	Well	**6**	Speaker
f	Lecterns	**6a**	Speaker pro Tempore
g	Round Table	**6b**	Chairman
		7a	Clerk of the House
		7b	Timekeeper
		8	Journal Clerk
		9	Tally Clerk
		10 & 11	Reading Enrolling Clerks
		12	Bill Clerk
		13	Enrolling "Digest" Office
		14	Clerks to the Official Reporters
		15–17	Official Reporters of Debates

THE HOUSE OF REPRESENTATIVES:
THE FLOOR

The Stage	*The Players*
e Well	**18** Representative
f Lecterns	
g Round Table	
h Benches	
i Aisle	
j Leadership and Committee Tables	
k Floor	
l Voting Stations	

front of an unruly member or even walk up and down the aisles carrying the mace in order to restore order in the chamber.

b. Speaker's Rostrum: The platform at the front of the House where the Speaker and the various officers and clerks of the House have their seats.

c. Clerk's Lectern: Desk at which the reading clerk stands.

d. Hopper: The box on the bill clerk's desk into which members place measures they are introducing.

e. Well: The area directly in front of the Speaker's rostrum.

f. Lecterns: The raised desks in the well of the House from which members speak. There are two, one on each side of the center aisle: (f_1), facing the Democratic seats, is used by members of the Democratic party; the other (f_2) faces the Republican seats and is used by members of that party.

g. Round Table: The worktable between the lecterns has places for two stenographers, the official reporters of debates.

h. Benches: The members' seats. They are placed in a semicircle facing the rostrum. Seats are not assigned, and although generally members choose to sit with their party, at times they do cross the aisle and sit with the opposition.

i. Aisle: The central aisle that divides the House chamber. As you face the Speaker's rostrum, Democrats are seated on the left, Republicans on the right. Members frequently refer to their colleagues "on the other side of the aisle."

j. Leadership and Committee Tables: The tables in back of the second row of each party's seats. They are used during debates by party leaders, committee chairs, and ranking members and by the staff of the committee whose bill is being considered. At the leadership tables are consoles that give information concerning a vote in progress. Members not wishing to address the House from the well may use the microphones at these tables.

k. Floor: The main section of the House chamber, the place where the members sit. Access is strictly limited.

l. Voting Stations: Boxlike devices attached to the backs of some of the benches and located throughout the chamber. Part of the electronic voting sytem, each has a blue light that signifies when it is open for use.

Not on diagram

Gallery: The gallery is above the chamber and provides seating for the press, the public, staff, and other visitors whenever the House is in session. Visitors are not allowed to take notes or pictures. Doorkeepers regulate what does and doesn't go on in the gallery. The gallery is not shown on normal C-SPAN television coverage.

Voting Display Panels: There are four display panels above and behind the Speaker's rostrum. They are part of the electronic voting system. Members are listed, and beside each name are lights to indicate how each has voted (red for nay; green for yea; amber for present). Summary display panels are on either side of the chamber. These identify the issue being voted upon and show running totals and the time remaining in which to vote.

THE PLAYERS—the People You See and Hear

1. Sergeant at Arms: The person in charge, under the direction of the Speaker, of maintaining order in the House and enforcing its rules. Either he or his deputy sits at a small table to the side of the rostrum. He is responsible for, among other things, the gallery and the Capitol Police. He has the power to "arrest" absent members (bring them to the chamber). In his keeping is the mace, the symbol of parliamentary power.

2–4. Pages: Young men and women (sixteen to eighteen years of age) who serve as messengers and floor assistants. They are patronage appointees and usually serve for six months to a year. They're under the direction of the sergeant at arms of the House. Five days a week pages attend a special school from six-ten to ten-thirty in the morning.

2. Speaker's Page: The page who serves the Speaker during the day's session.

3 and 4. Documentarian Pages: Pages who provide copies of all material needed during the day's session. They also carry material from the floor to the reading clerks. It's their job to operate the system of bells, buzzers, and lights that tell absent members what's happening on the chamber floor.

5. Parliamentarian: The expert on parliamentary rules of the House and the person to whom the presiding officer turns before making a ruling. Although appointed by the Speaker, the parliamentarian is nonpartisan and generally remains in office regardless of any change in the political control of the House.

6. Speaker: The presiding officer of the House. Although the full House votes for the Speaker, it is a pro forma election. Always elected by a straight party vote, the Speaker represents the majority party. Beginning with the 104th Congress, his tenure is limited to four consecutive Congresses. He is second in line behind the vice president to succeed to the presidency.

6a. Speaker pro Tempore: The person appointed by the Speaker to preside over the House in the Speaker's absence. The Speaker may appoint him to sit for any time up to three legislative days without approval by the House. Except in rare instances, the Speaker pro tem is of the majority party.

6b. Chairman: Person who presides when the House is sitting in the Committee of the Whole, the special committee that considers bills that raise or spend money. He is appointed by the Speaker.

7a. Clerk of the House: The House's chief administrative officer. He's nominated by the Speaker of the House and elected by the majority party of the chamber. He's responsible for the actual operation of the House—for example, taking votes, certification of bills, processing introduced legislation, and record keeping of daily debates and proceedings. Other clerks of the House having specific duties assist him and are considered extensions of his office.

7b. Timekeeper: Person who keeps track of and reports on time used during a debate or other business of the House. Although during a session he sits in the clerk of the House's seat, he is on the parliamentarian's staff.

8. Journal Clerk: The clerk responsible for keeping the *Journal*, the official record of the House's proceedings. An agent of the clerk of the House, he always sits at the extreme left of the middle level.

9. Tally Clerk: The clerk who supervises votes and quorum calls. He controls the electronic voting system via a computer terminal set into his area of the desk. He compiles members' individual voting records and the daily House Calendar. Conference and committee reports are filed with him. An agent of the clerk of the House, he sits to the left of the reading clerk's lectern.

10 and 11. Reading/Enrolling Clerks: The clerks who read aloud each matter of business brought to the floor of the House. They prepare the "true copy" of a bill, the final House version. They also serve as messengers to the Senate. Agents of the clerk of the House, they occupy the two seats to the right of the reading clerk's lectern.

12–14. Lower level of the Rostrum: Seats that are used at various times by the staffs of several offices involved in the record-keeping functions of the House.

12. Bill Clerk: The clerk in charge of the hopper, the box into which bills and resolutions are placed upon introduction. He also receives such items as lists of a measure's cosponsors and texts of amendments to be published in the *Congressional Record*. Every day he enters all legislative activity into LEGIS, a computer system that keeps track of a bill's progress through the legislative process. His is the last seat on the left on the lowest level.

13. Enrolling "Digest" Office: The office that keeps track of major House actions for the House "Digest." Its staff members use the seats to the left of center.

14. Clerks to the Official Reporters: Those who assemble a book that consists of all pieces of documentation—transcripts, speech texts, etc.—by number that make up the day's proceedings. These items are also incorporated into the *Congressional Record*. The clerks occupy the seats in the center.

15, 16, and 17. Official Reporters of Debates: Stenographers who take verbatim notes, which are used to prepare the accounts published in the *Congressional Record*. The House has seven reporters of debates. A reporter works a half hour shift, spending five minutes of each half hour on the floor and the remaining time dictating, transcribing, and correcting his notes. The reporters use devices similar to those used by court reporters. Their notes are immediately entered into a computer system that converts them into standard English. They are under the supervision of the clerk of the House and use the seats on the right of the lowest level in addition to the round table in the well.

18. Representative: One of 435 members, elected from districts in the fifty states apportioned by their total populations. Representatives must be at least twenty-five years old, citizens for at least seven years, and residents of the states, though not necessarily the districts, from which they are elected. They serve two-year terms beginning in odd-numbered years.

In addition to those representing the fifty states, there is a resident commissioner from Puerto Rico and delegates to the House from the District of Columbia, Guam, the Virgin Islands, and American Samoa. They may not vote on matters before the House but do vote in committee sessions.

Chaplain of the House: The spiritual counselor for the members, their families, and their staffs. Either he or a visiting clergyman offers a prayer each day before any House business is conducted.

Bench Pages: Pages who sit at the rear of the House. They distribute documents that will be needed during the day's session, answer cloakroom phones, and run errands. A member calls a page by pressing a button next to his seat that activates a light on a board at the rear of the House.

The Senate

THE STAGE—the Places and
Things You See
See diagrams pages 18 and 19.

a. Gavel: Mallet used by a presiding officer to gain a chamber's attention. Vice President John Adams is believed to have called the first Senate to order in 1789 with a handleless, silver-capped ivory gavel. The original disintegrated with age, and in 1954 the government of India replaced it with a replica. The original remains in a case on the rostrum.

b. Vice President's Rostrum: The platform at the front of the Senate where the presiding officer and other officers and clerks have their seats. Senate pages sit on the steps that run along the two sides of the rostrum.

c. Official Reporters' Tables: Two tables, with three seats each, that are assigned to the reporters who record material for the *Congressional Record*. The tables are, however, most often used by staffs of the majority and minority secretaries.

d. Desks: Their style is early nineteenth century, and each has an inkwell, a penholder, and a glass shaker filled with blotting sand. A new senator is assigned a desk in the rear of the chamber and moves toward the front as he gains seniority. The choicest desks are the ones closest to the front or nearest the center aisle. A microphone, activated as soon as it's picked up, is attached to each desk. Daniel Webster's desk is assigned to the senior New Hampshire senator, and Jefferson Davis's to the senior senator from Mississippi.

e. Desk of the Democratic Whip

f. Desk of the Democratic Leader

g. Desk of the Republican Leader

h. Desk of the Republican Whip
Majority and minority leaders are their party's chief strategists. The whips (Republicans call their whip the assistant leader) are the people who marshal the forces in support of those strategies. The majority and minority leaders face each other across the center aisle. Their desks are sometimes used by the majority and minority floor managers of a bill.

i. Lectern: Portable reading desk that a senator may place on top of his own desk. A lectern is brought by a page at a senator's request.

j. Floor: The Senate chamber. Access to it is strictly limited and controlled.

k. Center Aisle: The aisle that divides the Democratic and Republican parties. As you face the rostrum, Democrats sit to the left and Republicans to the right.

NOT ON DIAGRAM

Gallery: The area above the chamber that provides seating for the press, the public, staffs, and other visitors whenever the Senate is in session. Senators may not introduce or bring to the attention of the Senate during its sessions any person in the gallery. The gallery is not shown on normal C-SPAN coverage.

THE PLAYERS—the People You See and Hear

1. **Assistant Minority Secretary**
2. **Minority Secretary**
3. **Majority Secretary**
4. **Assistant Majority Secretary**

The minority and majority secretaries, their assistants, and staffs always sit facing their respective parties, and the titles Majority and Minority depend on their party's status in the chamber. Their main job is to help the party leaders manage the flow of legislation. They keep track of the action taking place on the floor, and a senator entering the chamber can consult with them to find out the day's schedule and the time he's expected to speak. The secretaries arrange pair votes and keep backup tallies on all votes. They assign seats to members of their respective parties and supervise the party cloakrooms. The secretaries are elected officers of the Senate, and their assistants are appointed.

5. **Sergeant at Arms:** The Senate's executive officer as well as law enforcement and protocol officer. Elected by the Senate, he has the power to locate and "arrest" absent members (bring them to the chamber), enforce

the chamber's rules and regulations, and direct the Senate's share of the Capitol Police. He plans such ceremonial events as inaugurations and funerals and escorts the U.S. president and visiting heads of state when they come to address Congress.

6. President of the Senate: The Constitution assigns the job of presiding officer of the Senate to the vice president of the United States. He presides, however, only on ceremonial occasions or when an issue important to the administration is being considered. He can cast his vote only when it's needed to break a tie.

6a. President of the Senate pro Tempore: Presiding officer in the absence of the vice president. He's nominated by the majority party caucus and is usually the party member with the longest continuous service. He holds office for as long as he's in the Senate or until the chamber chooses to hold another election. Like the vice president, he basically has a ceremonial role, but unlike the vice president, he may vote on all matters. He appoints members, usually from the majority party, to preside in his absence.

6b. Presiding Officer of the Senate: Person appointed by the president pro tem to chair the Senate as it goes about its day-to-day business. The job is rotated among majority-party members, each of whom sits for about one hour.

7. Secretary of the Senate: The Senate's chief administrative officer and custodian of its seal. He's nominated by the majority leader and elected by the majority party of the chamber. The secretary is responsible for the actual operation of the Senate: directing its employees, administering oaths, requisitioning funds for members' salaries and expenses, and certifying bills, treaty ratifications, and nominations.

8. *Journal* Clerk: The person responsible for keeping the Senate *Journal*, the official record of the chamber's proceedings. Senators give him the names of staff members they wish to have on the floor along with the dates, times, and purposes for their being there, so staff may be rotated if necessary to keep the chamber from becoming overcrowded.

9. Parliamentarian: The expert on the parliamentary rules of the Senate and the person who, acting for the president of the Senate, refers newly introduced bills to the appropriate committees. Appointed by the secretary of the Senate after consultation with the majority leader, he remains in office for as long as that party is in power. When the Senate is operating under a time constraint, he serves as its timekeeper.

10. Legislative Clerk: Person who prepares the Senate's legislative calendar, supervises all recorded votes and quorum calls, and acts as reading clerk, reading aloud any matter brought to the floor of the Senate.

11. Assistant Secretary of the Senate: Chief assistant to the secretary of the Senate. He performs the functions of the secretary in the latter's absence. His seat is usually occupied by one of the Senate clerks.

12. Pages: Young men and women (fourteen to sixteen years of age) who serve as messengers and floor assistants. They're appointed by senior members of each party under a distribution system directed by the majority leader and are supervised by the sergeant at arms. Those assigned to the floor sit on the steps to the side of the rostrum and a senator wishing one's services snaps his fingers. Five days a week pages attend a special school from six-ten to ten-thirty in the morning.

13. Official Reporters of Debates: Stenographers, appointed by the secretary of the Senate, who take verbatim notes, which are used to prepare the accounts published in the *Congressional Record*. They use devices similar to those used by court reporters. Their notes are immediately entered into a computer system that converts them into standard English. The Senate reporters operate on an hourly schedule, spending ten minutes of each hour on the floor and the remaining time dictating, transcribing, and correcting their notes. They carry their machines to stand near the senator who holds the floor.

14. Senator: One of one hundred members, two elected from each state regardless of its population. Senators must be at least thirty years old, citizens for at least nine years, and residents of the states electing them. They serve six-year terms with one third of the chamber elected every second year. The terms are such that the two senators coming from the same state are not up for election in the same year.

Shadow senators represent the District of Columbia and some U.S. territories. They don't participate in the Senate's business but spend most of their energy lobbying for statehood.

LESS FREQUENTLY SEEN

Chaplain of the Senate: The spiritual counselor for members, their families, and staffs. Either he or a visiting clergyman offers a prayer each day before any Senate business is conducted. He's escorted to the ros-

THE SENATE: THE PODIUM

The Stage

a Gavel
b Vice President's Rostrum
c Official Reporters' Tables

The Players

1 Assistant Minority Secretary
2 Minority Secretary
3 Majority Secretary
4 Assistant Majority Secretary
5 Sergeant at Arms
6 President of the Senate
6a President of the Senate pro Tempore
6b Presiding Officer of the Senate
7 Secretary of the Senate
8 *Journal* Clerk
9 Parliamentarian
10 Legislative Clerk
11 Assistant Secretary of the Senate
12 Pages
13 Official Reporters of Debates

THE SENATE: THE FLOOR

The Stage	*The Players*
b Vice President's Rostrum	**12** Pages
d Desks	**13** Official Reporters of Debates
e Desk of the Democratic Whip	**14** Senator
f Desk of the Democratic Leader	
g Desk of the Republican Leader	
h Desk of the Republican Whip	
i Lectern	
j Floor	
k Center Aisle	

trum by the secretary of the Senate and the sergeant at arms or their representatives.

Bill Clerk: The person who receives a measure after it has been numbered by the congressional record clerk. He enters its number, sponsors, and title into the Senate's computer-controlled data storage and retrieval system, LEGIS. The bill clerk keeps track of the legislative action taken on all Senate bills and resolutions and any House measures before the Senate. He prepares bills and reports for printing in the *Congressional Record* and provides committees with the printed official copies of measures that have been referred to them.

Doorkeeper: An agent of the sergeant at arms who looks after visitors to the Senate gallery.

Executive Clerk: The person who prepares the Executive Calendar and fulfills the same duties as the legislative clerk whenever executive business—a treaty or nomination—is being considered.

2

The Script

The Words You Hear and What They Mean

A.

Absence: See Leave of Absence.

Act: When the House or Senate passes a piece of legislation, a bill, the passed bill is then called an act. As the process continues and the act is passed by both chambers and signed by the president (or passed in spite of his veto), it's again given a more important label; it's now called a law.

Adjourn: To call it a day or, more to the point, officially to end a session or a legislative day. A motion to adjourn is of the highest priority, and a majority of those voting is what's needed to get it passed.

Adjournment to a Day Certain: Here the House or Senate decides to call a time out but sets the day and time of its next meeting. There's one catch: Neither chamber can adjourn for more than three days without the other's okay. Adjournment is accomplished by a concurrent resolution, a measure passed by both chambers that does not need the president's signature.

Adjournment sine Die (pronounced sine-ee die): Literally, adjournment "without a day." Here the House or Senate calls it quits without saying when it will meet again. It's accomplished by a concurrent resolution, a measure passed by both chambers that does not need the president's signature. The chambers usually do this to signal the final adjournment of a congressional session. It's time to go home.

Administrative Assistant (AA): See Personal Staff.

Advice and Consent: The Constitution gives the president the power to commit our country to treaties and to appoint ambassadors, other public ministers and consuls, justices of the Supreme Court, and other officers of the United States, but there's one catch: The president may do these things only if the Senate, after debating the issue, gives *its* approval. (See Confirmation.)

Amendment: A request to change the wording or essence of a bill by adding, substituting, or subtracting material. An amendment is usually printed in the *Congressional Record*, debated, and voted upon in the same way as is a bill.

There can be an amendment to an amendment (technically this means an amendment may be amended up to the second degree). And there may be a substitute for the original amendment, and, you guessed it, this too may be amended.

Amendments are voted upon in the following order: (1) an amendment to an amendment; (2) an amendment to the substitute; (3) the substitute for the amendment; (4) the amendment. If (3), the substitute, is agreed to, then the fourth vote is on the amendment as amended by the substitute. If the rule under which the bill is debated allows for an unlimited number of amendments, the process can seem to take forever. And don't be surprised if after voting aye on any number of amendments, the member then votes no on the bill. (See Amendment Procedure; Amendment in the Nature of a Substitute; Perfecting Amendment; Technical Amendment.)

Amendment in Disagreement: A pretty way to say an amendment upon which the House, Senate, or the members who make up a conference committee—a committee set up to reconcile differences in legislation passed by both chambers—can't agree.

The House or Senate first acts upon a conference report as a whole and after its adoption take up any amendments that have been reported in disagreement. A chamber may vote to eliminate its own amendment in disagreement—"to recede from it." Or to agree to it—"to concur with it." Or to concur with or concur with and amend an amendment in disagreement that originated in the other chamber. If an amendment in disagreement isn't disposed of, a further conference may be requested to deal with it.

Amendment in the Nature of a Substitute: This amendment is a way to replace the original text of a bill. When it strikes out (eliminates) everything that follows the enacting clause (the key phrase in a bill) or the resolving clause (the key phrase in a resolution) and substitutes entirely new language for them, it in fact rewrites the entire bill.

Amendment Procedure:
In the House: When general debate is over, amendments are taken up. They are offered and debated under the conditions set by the rule under which the bill is being considered. Amendments may be withdrawn only by unanimous consent. (See Rule; Five-Minute Rule.)

In the Senate: Once a bill has been brought to the floor, it's immediately open to unlimited amending, and the committee that brought the bill to the floor usually is the first to have its amendments considered. Sometimes a floor manager will agree to an amendment despite having reservations about it. He will say that he'll "take it to conference"—to the committee set up to reconcile differences in legislation passed by both chambers —even though he knows that it's very likely to die there. A sponsor may withdraw his amendment any time before action is taken upon it. (See Appropriation Bill; Appropriation Riders; Rider.)

Appeal: A challenge by a member to a chair's ruling. It's a plea to members to reverse the chair's decision. A majority vote is needed for it to succeed. This is a device commonly used in the Senate and rarely used in the House.

Appropriation Bill: An authorization bill gives a program the okay, but it still must be funded. The appropriation bill does just that. It grants money already approved by an authorization bill; it allows government agencies to take on obligations and to make payments out of the U.S. Treasury for specific purposes. It needn't grant the full amount called for in the authorization bill. An appropriation bill is the commonest form that budget authority takes.

In the Senate: In appropriation bills, amendments proposing new or general legislation and amendments increasing an appropriation by an amount not previously authorized or estimated for in the president's budget are not in order. Amendments that don't have anything to do with the bill's subject are also out of order. If the bill is about apples, the amendment can't be about oranges. (See Germane.)

Appropriation Riders: There are two kinds of amendment that may be tacked on to appropriation bills: (1) *Limitation riders*—they don't change existing law but restrict the use of appropriated monies. They are considered in keeping with the bill's subject matter in both chambers. (2) *Legislative riders*—they change existing law or add new duties to government agencies. In both chambers they are considered to have nothing to do with the bill's subject matter, and the rules must be waived by unanimous consent or by a two-thirds vote before they are agreed to. If the bill is about cows, the legislative rider can be about chickens. (See Germane.)

Architect of the Capitol: He's in charge of, among other things, the structural and mechanical care and maintenance of the Capitol Building. He's responsible as well for the care, maintenance, and improvement of the Capitol grounds, all 208.7 acres of them. He also makes arrangements with the proper authorities for ceremonies held in the building and on its grounds. The architect of the Capitol is appointed by the president.

Articles of Impeachment: These are accusations brought against a public official; they're much like an indictment in a criminal case. (See Impeach.)

In the House: Once articles of impeachment have been adopted by the House, they are taken to the Senate by specially appointed members called managers.

In the Senate: After a trial before the Senate, each article of impeachment is voted upon separately. A two-thirds vote of the members present is needed for a conviction.

Authorization Bill: This is a bill that sanctions—authorizes—a specific program—for example, WIC, a special program for women, infants, and children. It defines a program's aims and the way it will be run. Unless open-ended, the authorization bill puts a ceiling on the amount of money to be spent on the program. In 1992 WIC was budgeted for $2,597,000. Once a program has been okayed, it must be funded. (See Appropriation Bill.)

B.

Backdoor Spending: Government spending that bypasses the usual appropriations process. It's really okay despite what its name implies. (See Borrowing Authority; Contract Authority; Entitlement Program; Tax Expenditure.)

Balanced Budget Amendment: An amendment to the Constitution that would require the federal budget to be balanced in a designated number of years. It would mean that the government could no longer spend more than it took in.

Bells: See Legislative Call System.

Bill: A proposed law. Bills can be either public bills—those that deal with general matters—or private bills—those that deal with matters concerning an individual

—for example, specific immigration and naturalization cases. When passed by both House and Senate and signed by the president, or passed over his veto, a bill becomes either a public law or a private law. A bill that doesn't go on to become a law dies with the Congress in which it was introduced and must be reintroduced in the next Congress. In the House bills are designated "H.R." followed by a number; in the Senate "S." followed by a number.

Block Grants: Lump sums given to the states by the federal government for loosely defined purposes, such as child care or improving public safety.

Borrowing Authority: One of the forms that backdoor spending may take, it allows a government agency to borrow from either the U.S. Treasury or the public in order to finance a specific operation.

Bottle Up: To hold a bill in committee. This prevents the bill from reaching the floor for debate and potential passage.

Budget: A financial report estimating government revenue and expenditures (what comes in and what goes out) for the year beginning October 1 and ending September 30. Submitted to Congress by the president, it forms the basis for congressional action. Congress has the right to alter the budget to suit its own agenda, and it's rarely, if ever, passed without a lot of congressional tinkering.

Budget Authority: Legal provision for a government agency to take on obligations that require immediate or future payment of money. The basic forms it takes are appropriations, contract authority, and borrowing authority. Check them out.

Budget Resolution: A nonbinding measure passed by both chambers that sets out the congressional budget. It establishes various budget totals, divides spending totals into categories (for example, transportation), and may include reconciliation instructions to House or Senate committees.

By Request: Phrase to indicate that a member is introducing a measure at the request of others—the president, a special-interest group, a private organization, a government agency, you, or me. The member himself may or may not endorse the measure.

C.

Calendar: An agenda or list of business to come. After a bill has been reported out by a committee of the House or Senate, it is placed on a calendar and given a calendar number. Bills may not necessarily come to the floor for action in chronological order. It's the House Rules Committee and the majority leader of the Senate that decide the order of business.

In the House: Here there are five separate legislative calendars: the Consent Calendar, Corrections Calendar, House Calendar, Private Calendar, Union Calendar as well as a Discharge Calendar. There is also a single cumulative calendar, the Calendars of the U.S. House of Representatives and History of Legislation. All are printed daily.

In the Senate: Here there are two calendars: the Calendar of Business and the Executive Calendar.

Calendar of Business (General Orders): The legislative calendar of the Senate, published daily by the legislative clerk. It lists all bills and resolutions reported by committees, as well as some bills already passed by the House. Senators can bypass the committee system by introducing measures and having them placed directly on this calendar. (See Call of the Calendar.)

Calendar Wednesday: Each Wednesday the standing House committees are called in alphabetical order, from A to W: Agriculture to Ways and Means. At that time a committee may bring up from the House or Union Calendar a measure that hasn't yet received a rule from the Rules Committee concerning the conditions under which it will be debated and amended. General debate on the measure is limited to two hours, equally divided between those for and against. A simple majority of those present is enough for passage. Calendar Wednesday may be dispensed with by a two-thirds vote and is not observed during the last two weeks of a session.

Calendars of the U.S. House of Representatives and History of Legislation: This calendar is printed every day that Congress is in session. Along with a listing of all the bills on the five legislative calendars of the House, it gives capsule legislative histories of all measures reported by House and Senate standing committees.

Call of the Calendar: Senate bills that haven't been brought to the floor by a motion or by a unanimous consent agreement may come up for action when the Calendar of Business is called. Although the calendar may be called on any day at the conclusion of morning business and is given top priority on Monday, it's usually called only once or twice a month. The majority leader decides the order in which bills on the calendar should come to the floor. A measure brought on the call of the calendar is generally noncontroversial, but if an objection to its consideration is raised, the measure is passed over unless a motion to consider is adopted. On bills brought on the call of the calendar each senator is limited to five minutes of debate on the bill and five minutes on each amendment to it.

Call of the House: When a quorum isn't present, fifteen members, including the Speaker, can order the attendance of absent members. Calls of the House are almost always taken by electronic device, and members are given fifteen minutes to record their presence. If a member's absence is not excused, the majority present may order the sergeant at arms to "compel" the member's attendance. (See Leave of Absence.)

Campaign Committees: Set up by both House and Senate Republicans and Democrats, they raise funds for election campaigns. Individuals may also set up their own campaign committees. (See PAC.)

Caucus: A group of like-minded people. Party caucuses are formal organizations of Democrats and Republicans that usually decide such matters as procedures, rules, and assignments. Alliances may also be formed across party lines to develop policies on issues important to a member or to his constituents—for example, the Congressional Black Caucus. Senate and House Republicans, as well as Senate Democrats, formally use the word "conference" instead of "caucus."

Censure: A formal procedure where a chamber may sharply criticize a member who it believes was involved in wrongdoing. A member who's been censured doesn't lose his seat, committee assignments, or seniority, but it's a very serious matter, and he does take notice, and so do the people he represents. It takes a majority vote to censure. (See Expulsion; Reprimand.)

Chair: The place from which a presiding officer operates as well as the term used to indicate such a person. For example, it's from the chair that the chair presides over the Committee of the Whole House.

Chamber: The place where either the full House or Senate meets. It's usually used to mean the House or Senate itself.

Christmas Tree Bill: A minor measure passed by the House to which the Senate has added a number of special-interest amendments that have nothing to do with the bill. The amendments are like decorations hung from a Christmas tree, which explains the name. (See Pork Barrel; Rider.)

Class: Members of Congress that share a specific term of office.
In the House: The class is designated by the year each member was elected—the class of '84, the class of '98, etc.
In the Senate: The Constitution divides the Senate into three classes. One third of the members, one class, is elected every second year.

Clean Bill: A spanking new bill, one that combines the changes made by a committee with what is left of the original bill. It's usually put together by a committee member. It's a time-saver because the committee-recommended changes don't then have to be considered one at a time. Clean bills are given new House or Senate numbers.

Cloakrooms: Two rooms at the rear of the House and Senate. Each party oversees the cloakroom on its side of the chamber. They once were where members left their hats and coats, but they now serve as private member lounges. The cloakrooms are places where members may meet to discuss legislation, make telephone calls, or simply rest.

Closed Rule: Ordered by the House Rules Committee, this is one type of resolution setting out how an upcoming bill will be handled on the House floor. It allows amendments proposed by the committee reporting the bill but prohibits anyone else from offering an amendment.

Closed Session: See Secret Session.

Cloture: Rule XXII of the *Senate Manual*, it's the way the Senate can end a filibuster. To be filed, a petition for cloture must have the signatures of at least sixteen senators. A vote can be taken one calendar day after the filing of a petition. To stop debate on regular measures, a majority vote of three fifths (sixty) of all senators is needed. For measures concerning a change in the Senate rules, a two-thirds vote is needed. Once cloture has been invoked, there is a thirty-hour cap on all action concerning the measure. However, the thirty hours may be increased by the adoption of a motion by a three-fifths affirmative vote. (See Filibuster.)

COLA: An acronym for "cost of living adjustment." Through the use of a COLA, additional budget authority is given to such entitlement programs as Social Security.

Colloquy: A dialogue. A member may yield to or take time to be questioned by another member about the exact meaning of a measure. Colloquies become part of a measure's legislative history and help make clear what the chamber had in mind when it debated a piece of legislation.

Comity: Courtesy. (See Decorum.)

Commemorations: Pieces of legislation that honor certain special products or ideas—for example, National Pickle Week.
In the House: The 104th Congress did away with such legislation.

Committee: A working subdivision of the House or Senate that prepares legislation or conducts investigations; committees and their subcommittees have specific areas of concern. Assignments are made by the individual parties and approved by their caucuses and by pro forma elections held in the full House and Senate. Committee members' rank depends on the order in which they are appointed to the committee. The chairs are elected from nominees submitted by the majority-party caucus at the start of each Congress. With few exceptions, committees in both the House and Senate must get special permission to meet while their chamber is in session. (See Subcommittee; Joint Committee; Select or Special Committee; Standing Committee; Conference Committee; Oversight Committee; Multiple Referral.)
In the House: Members aren't allowed more than two full committee assignments and four subcommittee as-

signments. Beginning with the 104th Congress, no member can serve as a chair of a standing committee for more than three consecutive Congresses. The results of roll call votes are available to the public. Also available are descriptions of amendments, motions, and orders voted upon and the names of each member voting for and against, as well as those not voting. Beginning with the 104th Congress, "except in extraordinary circumstances" all meetings and hearings are open to the public and may be broadcast.

In the Senate: A senator may not chair more than one standing, select, or special committee or subcommittee. Beginning in 1997, committee and subcommittee chairs will be limited to six-year terms.

Committee Calendar: Senate committees periodically publish a calendar that lists the bills and resolutions referred to them, the action taken upon these measures, and other relevant information.

Committee of the Whole: The House or Senate sitting as a committee; one having its own chair, set of rules, and special purpose.

In the House: Bills that raise or spend money must be considered in the Committee of the Whole, where only one hundred members are needed for a quorum. The Speaker can turn the House into the Committee of the Whole without a vote. Having done so, he appoints a member of the majority party to preside over the committee as its chair. When the committee's work is concluded, it returns to regular session (resolves itself) by rising, and the Speaker returns. The chair leaves the Speaker's platform and reports the committee's recommendation: passage or rejection of a measure. The full House then acts.

When the mace (the symbol of authority) is moved

from the pedestal at the right of the Speaker's desk to a low marble pedestal farther to the right, it tells members that the House is sitting in the Committee of the Whole. (See Five-Minute Rule.)

In the Senate: Treaties are the only business the Senate considers in the Committee of the Whole. Any amendments adopted in the committee are also voted upon by the Senate.

Committee of the Whole House on the State of the Union: In the House this is the formal name of the Committee of the Whole.

Committee Print: Material published by a committee. Committees publish for various purposes. For example, the rules of a standing committee, drafts of bills, or committee reports may be produced as committee prints.

Committee Staff: Aides whose jobs include organizing hearings, drafting amendments, doing original research, preparing reports to accompany bills, and preparing conference reports. A limited number of staff members are allowed on the floor during consideration of their committee's business. (See Personal Staff.)

In the House: There is no distinction between professional and clerical staff. There can't be more than thirty committee staff members, and the minority is entitled to one third of them.

In the Senate: The minority is entitled for its staff to one third of the funds that aren't allocated to pay administrative and clerical functions.

Companion Bill: A bill introduced in one chamber that is almost identical to one introduced in the other.

Concurrent Budget Resolution: A nonbinding measure that sets target figures for the congressional budget, for both spending and revenue.

Concurrent Resolution: A form of legislation used to amend rules affecting the operation of both the House and Senate—for example, setting the time of adjournment. It's also used to give the "sense of Congress"—that is, to express both chambers' joint feelings on a matter. An example might be voicing this country's dislike of another nation's actions. Concurrent resolutions must be passed by both chambers but don't need the president's signature and don't have the force of law. In the House they are designated "H. Con. Res." followed by a number; in the Senate, "S. Con. Res." followed by a number. (See Concurrent Budget Resolution.)

Conditional Adjournment: When Congress adjourns for more than three days, a concurrent resolution may authorize it to reconvene at an earlier date in order to address an emergency or important issue.

Conference Committee: A committee made up of House and Senate members (called managers) whose job it is to settle matters of disagreement. Because the president can only be sent a bill that has passed both House and Senate in identical form, when neither chamber is willing to accept the other's amendments, a conference is requested. The conference committee doesn't consider provisions already agreed to, nor does it add any new material.

Each of a bill's provisions must be agreed to by a majority of the House managers and a majority of the Senate managers. If they fail to agree, they may return to their chambers for instruction or simply report their failure and allow the House and Senate to proceed as they wish—for example, call for another conference or make changes in the bill.

Conference committees are open to the public except when a majority of the managers, in open session and by a roll call vote of those present, agree to close all or part of the remainder of the meeting on the day of the vote. (See Amendment in Disagreement; Conference Report; Selection of Conferees; Instructions to Conferees.)

In the House: If the conference committee fails to report within twenty calendar days, a motion may be made to discharge the House conferees, to appoint new ones, or to give them special instructions concerning how they may proceed.

Conference Report: The compromise bill fashioned by a conference committee, it's signed by a majority of conferees from each chamber. Both House and Senate vote on the report without any further amendments. If one or the other rejects the report, a new conference may be called or another bill introduced. (See Amendment in Disagreement.)

Confirmation: An informal term for the Senate's giving its advice and consent to a presidential nomination.

Congressional Budget Office (CBO): Support agency that provides Congress with basic budget data, it's the legislative counterpart of the president's Office of Management and Budget, and the Council of Economic Advisers. Among other things, the CBO prepares five-year cost estimates of proposed legislation, assesses the inflationary impact of bills, analyzes and forecasts economic trends, and takes a long hard look at the president's annual budget. Through it all the

CBO is meant to remain impartial, siding with neither political party.

Congressional Record: The daily verbatim printed account of congressional proceedings. Members may, however, revise and edit their remarks before publication. The *Record* consists of four separate parts: (1) "Proceedings of the House"; (2) "Proceedings of the Senate"; (3) "Extension of Remarks"; and (4) "Daily Digest." (See "Extension of Remarks"; "Daily Digest".)

Congressional Research Service (CRS): A support agency located in the Library of Congress that serves all members, committees, and staff aides. Among other things it researches specific requests, publishes digests of bills and briefs on topics of general legislative interest, translates members' official correspondence from or into a foreign language as needed, provides charts for presentation of statistics, and has telephone hot lines from the House and Senate floors to answer questions during debates.

Consent Calendar: The House agenda of noncontroversial bills already on the Union and House calendars. It's called on the first and third Mondays of each month, and the bills are passed by unanimous consent, without objection or debate. If there is an objection the first time a bill is called, it is carried over to the next day the Consent Calendar is called. If there are three objections the second time it's called, the bill is stricken from the Consent Calendar but remains on the Union and House calendars. When a member asks that a bill be passed over "without prejudice," no objection is recorded, and it remains on the Consent Calendar.

Its consideration is merely postponed until the next time the calendar is called. (See Objectors.)

Constitutional Amendment: A two-thirds vote of both chambers is needed for Congress to propose an amendment to the U.S. Constitution. The amendment must then be ratified by three fourths of the states.

Contempt of Congress: It's an offense to try to throw a monkey wrench into the legislative process by refusing to give information for which Congress has asked. Congress can issue a contempt citation against anyone who refuses to testify or produce required evidence. Congress may try contempt cases itself, turn them over to the Department of Justice, or file civil charges, which puts the matter into the hands of a federal judge. A person found guilty of contempt of Congress may face a prison sentence.

Continuing Resolution: Legislation that gives budget authority for specific ongoing activities, it's used when Congress hasn't yet passed all regular appropriation bills at the beginning of the fiscal year (October 1). Passed jointly by the House and Senate, the continuing resolution is usually based on the previous year's appropriations.

Contract Authority: One form of backdoor spending. It gives budget authority for a government agency to obligate funds (e.g., enter into contracts) that require future appropriations.

Control the Time: A member having the floor for a specified amount of time may determine what's to be done with it. He may use the time himself or give it to another.

In the House: The floor managers yield specific amounts of time for debate. Although a member thus gaining the floor may in turn yield part of his time to another, he has the right to reclaim his time whenever he wishes.

In the Senate: If no limit has been imposed by a unanimous consent agreement, a senator may speak twice on the same subject during any legislative day for as long as he likes. Because of this rule, floor managers yield time but do not specify the amount of time yielded.

Correcting the Record: To change his vote, even months after it was cast, or to correct errors in the text of the *Congressional Record*, a member must first announce that he was "incorrectly recorded." If unanimous consent is obtained, he may then make any changes he wishes.

In the House: Votes may be changed only if they were taken by roll call and not by the electronic voting system.

Corrections Calendar: A bill that's been placed on the Union or House calendar may, upon request of the Speaker (after consulting with the minority leader), be placed on the Corrections Calendar. It's called on the second and fourth Tuesdays of each month and is a fast-track procedure under which measures to repeal federal regulations thought unnecessary or ill advised may be taken up. A three-fifths vote of the members voting is needed for passage, and if a bill is rejected, it can be returned to its original calendar.

Corrections Day:
In the House: The second and fourth Tuesdays of each month, the time when the Corrections Calendar is taken up.

C-SPAN: The Cable Satellite Public Affairs Network. A nonprofit cooperative of the cable TV industry, it provides public affairs programming to the national cable TV audience. The first order of its programming is gavel-to-gavel coverage of both the House and Senate.

𝒟.

"Daily Digest": The part of the *Congressional Record* that gives summaries of floor and committee actions of both House and Senate. It includes a calendar of committee meetings scheduled for the next day.

"Dear Colleague" Letter: A letter circulated to members asking for their participation. It often asks members to cosponsor a bill.

Decorum: "Decorum" is another way of saying "etiquette," "comity" is another way of saying "courtesy," and both are practiced by Congress. During debates the language members use is extremely polite and old-fashioned. For example, following House and Senate rules, members must address the presiding officer rather than each other. In the House it is "Mr. Speaker," and in the Senate, "Mr. President." There are additional taboos along these lines. For example, during a House session no member may wear his hat, walk out while another is speaking, or use a cellular phone or computer. (See Other Body; Words Taken Down.)

Deferral: A tactic used by the president to delay the spending of funds already appropriated. His deferral stands unless it's overturned by a resolution of either chamber. (See Rescission.)

Deficiency Appropriation: See Supplemental Appropriation.

Deputy President pro Tempore: Senate office created in 1977. It's held by any member of the Senate who has been either president or vice president of the United States. Neither the duties nor the responsibilities of the office are specified.

Dilatory Motion: A motion proposed for the obvious purpose of blocking a chamber's business, it's forbidden in both House and Senate. Enforcement of the rules against such motions is, however, chiefly in the hands of the chair.

Discharge a Committee: To excuse a committee from doing any more work on a measure it has before it.
In the House: To expedite noncontroversial business, a committee may be discharged by unanimous consent of the House. But measures that have been bottled up in committee are a different story. (See Discharge Petition.)
In the Senate: Although this device is rarely used, a senator may have a committee discharged by offering a motion to discharge. If it's passed, the bill in question is placed on the Calendar of Business. The far more common way for the Senate to bring a bill to the floor if it has been bottled up in committee is to offer it as a floor amendment to a pending measure. (See Discharge Resolution; Rider.)

Discharge Calendar: Officially entitled the Calendar of Motions to Discharge Committees. This is the House calendar of written motions to release committees from further consideration of bills. Discharge motions are taken up on the second and fourth Mondays of each month, except during the last six days of a session.

Discharge Petition:

In the House: A seldom used and complicated way to bring to the floor a measure that's been bottled up in committee for more than thirty days. A written motion or petition to discharge a committee requires 218 signatures in order to be placed on the Discharge Calendar. It remains on the calendar for seven days (thus giving the committee time to act) before it's considered by the House. At that point any member who has signed the petition may move that the committee be discharged from its consideration of the measure before it. Debate on the motion is limited to twenty minutes, divided equally between those for and against. If the motion carries, the bill becomes a matter of high privilege and may be either considered immediately or placed on one of the calendars.

Discharge Resolution:

In the Senate: During the morning hour any senator may offer a motion to discharge a committee. After being held for one legislative day the motion can be voted on, and it needs a simple majority for passage. The procedure is little used, however.

Discretionary Spending: Spending (budget authority and outlays) controlled in annual appropriations acts.

District Work Period: The Christmas, Thanksgiving, or other holiday recess when House members go home to their districts. Time at home is spent meeting with constituents and just plain having fun.

Division of a Question: Subject to certain restrictions, this motion allows the separation of a question into its distinct parts. Each part may then be considered and voted upon.

Division (Standing) Vote: One kind of nonrecorded vote. Here members in favor are asked to stand and be counted by the chair. When they are seated, members who are opposed are asked to stand and be counted.
In the House: The chair announces the number voting for and the number voting against.
In the Senate: The chair announces only the result of the vote—whether the measure being voted upon has passed or not. The actual vote count is not reported. One fifth of the senators present (but at least eleven) may demand a roll call vote before the result of a division vote is announced.

E.

Electronic Voting System: Used only in the House, it allows members to use IDs about the size of credit cards to vote. Voting stations are attached to the backs of some seats in the chamber; a member inserts the card and presses one of the three buttons to indicate a vote of yea, nay, or present. A card may be reinserted to change or verify a vote. If a member doesn't have his card, he may use a paper ballot: green for "yea," red for "nay," amber for "present." This ballot is given to the tally clerk, who records the vote electronically. Four display panels on the walls of the chamber list members by name; beside each name are colored lights that correspond to the way the member has voted.

Enacting Clause: "Be it enacted by the Senate and House of Representatives of the United States in Congress assembled . . ." is the key phrase at the beginning of every bill. A successful motion to strike the enacting clause kills the bill. (See Resolving Clause.)

En Bloc: "En masse" or "taken together." The Senate, when dealing with noncontroversial resolutions, treaties, or nominations, may vote for them as a group rather than take a vote on each measure separately. (See In Gross.)

Engrossed Bill: The final copy of a bill (including all amendments) as it has been passed by the House or Senate. At this point it's time for the other chamber to go to work on the legislation, and the bill, now technically an act of the House or Senate, is delivered to it for its consideration.
In the House: An engrossed bill is printed on blue paper and certified by the clerk of the House.
In the Senate: An engrossed bill is printed on special white paper and certified by the secretary of the Senate.

Enrolled Bill: Final copy of a bill that has been passed in identical form by both chambers. The enrolling clerk in the chamber that originally presented the measure prepares the bill, which is printed on parchment. It's certified as correct by an officer in that chamber and then sent on for signatures of the Speaker of the House (who always signs first) and the Senate president before being sent to the president for his signature.

Entitlement Program: A form of backdoor spending. It's a program with mandatory outlays—that is, the government is obligated to give benefits to those people who meet certain criteria. Entitlement programs include Social Security, food stamps, and veterans' disability benefits.

Executive Calendar: The Senate's agenda for nonlegislative business—treaties and presidential nominations—that have been reported by committees. It's published daily by the executive clerk.

Executive Documents: Communications from the executive branch of the government, including treaties and presidential nominations that are sent to the Senate for its consideration. Documents are given message numbers and referred to the appropriate Senate committees.

Executive Privilege: A president's right to refuse to give Congress executive branch documents for which it has asked. Presidents have argued for this right based on the fact that they head a separate branch of the government. The Supreme Court found that certain material could be withheld but not from a criminal investigation. (See Subpoena Power.)

Executive Session:
In the Senate: The time when the Senate deals with matters on the Executive Calendar—treaties and nominations.

Ex Officio: Literally, "by virtue of one's office." Senate rules allow committee chairs and ranking minority members to participate in any of the subcommittees of their committees, but generally not to vote.

Expulsion: This is the most severe form of disciplining a member. A chamber may expel a member it believes was involved in wrongdoing. It takes a two-thirds vote to expel. Fourteen senators and three representatives were expelled for supporting the South's rebellion (the Civil War). (See Censure; Reprimand.)

"Extension of Remarks": The section of the *Congressional Record* into which members may place additional or extraneous material—usually speeches given outside Congress, selected editorials, magazine articles, or letters. Any material not actually delivered during debate is set off by bullets (●●●) or by the use of a DIFFERENT TYPEFACE. When the material exceeds two printed pages, the member must give an estimate of how much the printing will cost.
In the House: Members must ask unanimous consent that they be allowed to add material to this section of the *Congressional Record*.
In the Senate: Members may choose to place such extraneous material in the body of the *Congressional Record*.

F.

Filibuster: Unlimited debate. It's used in the Senate to block the passage of a bill. Teamwork is often required as a group of senators holds the floor for days and even weeks. Of course, individual senators can filibuster. South Carolina's Strom Thurmond holds the record. He once held the floor for more than twenty-four hours in an attempt to block civil rights legislation. A filibuster may be stopped by the adoption of a cloture motion.

Fiscal Year: The year between one reckoning of accounts and another. The fiscal year of the U.S. government runs from October 1 through September 30 and carries the date of the calendar year in which it ends. For example, fiscal year 1996 began on October 1, 1995, and ended on September 30, 1996.

Five-Minute Rule:
In the House: The rule under which the Committee of the Whole considers an amendment. It allows a sponsor five minutes to explain and defend an amendment and gives an equal five minutes to a member who is recognized to speak against it.

Floor Managers: The two members whose job it is to steer a bill through to final decision. They're usually the chair and the ranking minority member of the committee or subcommittee reporting the bill.
In the House: Floor managers sit at the large tables in back of the second row of each party's seats. They open and close debate and are responsible for allocating time to others during the debate. When both are in favor of the measure, a member who doesn't agree may demand one third of the time.
In the Senate: Floor managers move up to sit at the leader's front-row desks. Before debate begins on the amendments to a bill, the presiding officer recognizes both the majority and minority floor managers for brief statements. Unless the Senate is operating under the rules of a unanimous consent agreement that states otherwise, each senator is permitted to speak twice on the same subject during any legislative day. Because he may speak as long as he likes, there is no need for floor managers to parcel out time for debate.

Floor Privileges: Only certain people are allowed onto the floor of the House and Senate. They include, of course, the members, their staffs, and committee staffs. Also allowed are the president and vice president, cabinet members, Supreme Court justices, governors, the architect of the Capitol, senior military officers, and the mayor of the District of Columbia. Former members are barred from the floor during any debate or vote on a bill in which they have personal or business interests.

Franking Privilege: On certain letters and packages, mail goes free—that is, a member's facsimile signature may be used instead of stamps.

G.

General Accounting Office (GAO): A support agency that acts as Congress's watchdog over government spending. Its chief functions are: (1) to initiate audits and review agencies and programs; (2) to set up accounting standards; (3) to provide legal opinions, usually regarding an agency's authority to spend public funds; (4) to settle claims by or against the government; and (5) to fulfill congressional requests for special investigative reports. The GAO is headed by the comptroller general of the United States.

General Debate: The discussion of a bill or resolution on the chamber floor.
In the House: The amount of time allowed for general debate is specified in the rule under which the measure is being considered and is equally divided between those for and those against. When general debate is concluded, the process of amending, if permitted under the rule, begins.

General Pair: See Pairing of Members.

Germane: Pertaining to the subject matter under discussion, for example, amendments to a bill concerning fishing can be about nets.

In the House: All amendments must be germane to the bill, or they won't be considered.

In the Senate: Amendments don't have to be germane except in general appropriation bills, bills on which cloture has been invoked, concurrent budget resolutions, or measures regulated by a unanimous consent decree that insists on germaneness. However, on appropriation bills a motion to permit consideration of an amendment, if passed by a two-thirds majority vote, may permit nongermaneness. (See Nongermane Amendment; Rider.)

Gerrymandering: A way of drawing district lines. It deliberately favors one party's candidates over the others.

Government Printing Office (GPO): This office carries out the printing and binding orders placed by Congress and departments of the federal government. It supplies paper and ink. It prepares catalogs and distributes and sells government publications. It's headed by the public printer, who the law says must be a practical printer versed in the art of bookbinding. He's appointed by the president with the advice and consent of the Senate.

Grandfather Clause: A clause exempting certain people, those already engaged in an activity, when that activity is about to be restricted by new legislation. If, in 1995, air bags are required in cars, you won't need one if the car you're now driving was bought in 1985. You've been "grandfathered."

$\mathscr{H}$.

Hearing: A committee session in which witnesses are called. Hearings are generally held first by a subcommittee in order to decide whether a bill is worth taking up in the full committee. Later the full committee may itself decide to hold hearings.

Sometimes witnesses are placed under oath. Traditionally a witness begins by summarizing his written statement, which has already been submitted to the committee. Next, each committee member is allowed a limited time for asking questions. Witnesses receive per diem rates as well as actual travel expenses.

In the House: Hearings (and committee meetings) are open to the public "except in extraordinary circumstances." The "sunshine" resolution, passed in 1995, assures the right to broadcast coverage of any hearing or meeting open to the public.

In the Senate: Hearings may only be closed for some few very specific reasons stated in the rules. The closing of a hearing requires a majority vote of the members, taken in open session.

Holds:

In the Senate: A senator may ask the party leaders to place a hold on a bill—that is, to put off action on it. It's an informal arrangement sometimes used as a bargaining chip and may be lifted at any time by the party leadership or at the request of the senator who requested it in the first place.

House Calendar: In the House the agenda of public bills that are not concerned with raising or spending money. These bills are usually dealt with by the House itself, not by the Committee of the Whole.

𝒥.

Impeach: To charge a federal official, and that includes the president, with misbehaving in office. The Constitution gives the House the power of impeachment and the Senate the power to try all impeachments. (See Articles of Impeachment; Manager.)

In the House: An impeachment may be set in motion in various ways. Charges may be made on the floor by a member, in a message from the president, in a memorial, or by a resolution dropped into the hopper, or they may be transmitted from a state legislature or a grand jury or based on facts developed and reported by an investigation committee of the House.

In the Senate: In recent years the Senate has set up a special committee to hear evidence in an impeachment case. The committee reports its findings to the full Senate, which then rules on the matter.

Impoundment of Funds: It's now illegal for a president to withhold money that's been appropriated by Congress. However, there are still steps a president may take if he doesn't like a project for which funds have been designated. (See Deferral; Rescission.)

Independents: Neither Republicans nor Democrats, third-party or independent candidates are rarely elected to the House and Senate. If elected, an independent usually joins one of the party conferences in order to receive such things as committee assignments. In a closely divided chamber an independent's vote may tip the scales.

In Gross: "En masse" or "taken together." When the full House considers amendments adopted in the Committee of the Whole, separate votes may be demanded.

Those amendments upon which separate votes are not asked are voted upon together by pro forma voice vote. (See En Bloc.)

Inspector General: He's appointed by the Speaker and the House majority and minority leaders acting together. His job is to conduct a comprehensive audit of House financial records, physical assets, and operational facilities.

Instructions to Conferees: Both the House and Senate may pass guidelines for their conferees. These instructions may concern such things as specific language or spending levels that the chamber wishes to see included in the final bill. Although not binding, such instructions do give a sense of how much the chamber cares about a given issue.

Introduction of a Bill: Placing a measure into the legislative process. It's the beginning of a bill's journey on the road to becoming a law.
In the House: Any member may introduce a bill at any time by simply placing it in the hopper, the box at the bill clerk's desk. The bill's title is entered in the *Journal* and printed in the *Congressional Record*. The clerk next assigns the bill its designation number and passes it along to the Speaker, who, with the help of the parliamentarian, assigns it to the appropriate committee. The Speaker may refer the matter to one or more committees for consideration in sequence but must designate a committee to have primary jurisdiction.
In the Senate: A senator may introduce a bill from the floor at any time, but he most often does so by handing it in at the clerk's desk. After the measure has been given its designation number, the parliamentarian, acting for the president of the Senate, refers the bill to the

appropriate committee. Referral to two or more committees may be done jointly or sequentially.

J.

Jefferson's Manual: In 1801 Vice President Thomas Jefferson published his *Manual of Parliamentary Practice.* This handbook is still part of the House rules manual.

Joint Committee: A committee that includes members from both House and Senate. Chairmanship rotates between House and Senate members. Some, such as the Joint Economic Committee and the Joint Library Committee, are standing (permanent) committees; others are temporary panels set up to study and investigate specific issues.

Joint Meeting: An occasion when the House and Senate meet together. Business is not in order because both chambers are in recess at this time. Visiting foreign dignitaries may address a joint meeting. (See Joint Session.)

Joint Resolution: One of the forms legislation may take. It's generally used to deal with limited matters—for example, a single appropriation for a specific purpose. There's no real difference between it and a bill, and like a bill, it requires approval by both chambers and the president before becoming law.

A joint resolution is also used to propose an amendment to the Constitution. Here it's not given to the president for his approval but, after passing both chambers, is sent directly to the administrator of general services for submission to the states.

Whatever its purpose, in the House it's designated "H. J. Res." followed by a number; in the Senate, "S. J. Res." followed by a number.

Joint Session: An occasion when the House and Senate meet together for a specific purpose—for example, to hear an address by the president. (Only the president may address a joint session.) Because both chambers are in session during this time, in theory congressional business could be conducted at a joint session. (See Joint Meeting.)

Journals: Both House and Senate keep *Journals*, the official records of each chamber's proceedings, ordered by the Constitution. The *Journals* are anything but long-winded and don't include verbatim reports of speeches, debates, etc. They list such things as newly introduced bills and resolutions, which committees got what, what amendments were offered, and what votes were taken. (See Congressional Record.)

In the House: At the opening of each daily session, the Speaker, having read the *Journal* of the prior day's happenings, announces his approval of it. The House votes on whether to accept that approval. The Speaker may postpone a recorded vote on the *Journal* until later on the same legislative day.

In the Senate: Except when the Senate is operating under the rule of cloture, the preceding day's *Journal* is read and approved at the start of each daily session. Reading can be suspended only by unanimous consent. Senate rules also order that different *Journals* be kept for legislative and executive proceedings (treaties and nominations), as well as for confidential legislative proceedings and proceedings when the Senate sits as a court for impeachment.

Junior Senator: The senator with the least seniority of the two representing a single state. (See Senior Senator.)

Junket: A trip taken by a member at the government's expense. The word implies that the trip may have been for pleasure rather than business.

Lame-Duck Session: A session held after the November elections and before January, the beginning of the new Congress. Retiring members or members who have not been reelected can attend this postelection session and vote, but their influence is very limited. Lame-duck sessions are held rarely and then only to complete important outstanding legislation.

Law: An act of Congress that has been signed by the president or passed over his veto.

Lay on the Table: See Table.

Layover:
In the Senate: An informal term for a period of delay required by rule. For example, when a bill is reported from committee, it may be considered on the floor only after it lies over for one legislative day and after the written report has been available for two calendar days. Layover periods may be waived by unanimous consent.

Leave of Absence: No member may be absent from either the House or the Senate without permission of the chamber.
In the House: A request for a leave of absence is filed on a printed form. Requests are read out by the clerk and usually granted by general consent. On rare occasions they may be opposed or even refused. (See Call of the House.)

Leave to Sit: Permission for a committee to meet during the proceeding of its chamber.

In the Senate: Under Rule XXVI, committees are forbidden to meet after the first two hours of the Senate's daily session, and in no case after 2:00 P.M. while the Senate is in session, unless they have special permission from the majority and minority leaders.

Legislative Assistant (LA): See Personal Staff.

Legislative Call System: Bells, buzzers, and lights in the Capitol and House and Senate office buildings that're used to alert members to what's going on in the two chambers.

In the House: Some combinations are more complex than others. For example, three bells and three lights indicate a quorum call either in the House or in the Committee of the Whole by electronic system or by clerks. The bells are repeated five minutes after they first ring. When the quorum call is by call of the roll, three bells are followed by a brief pause, then by three more bells, with the process repeated when the clerk reaches the *R*'s in the first call of the roll. Here are some simpler ones: Four bells and four lights signal an adjournment, and five bells and five lights any five-minute vote.

In the Senate: One bell signifies a roll call vote; two, a quorum call; three, a call of absentees; four, an adjournment or recess; and five that there are seven and a half minutes left on a yea and nay vote. More complex combinations of bells and lights signal other Senate business.

Legislative Day: The "day" extends from the time the House or Senate meets after an adjournment until it next adjourns.

In the House: Legislative days and calendar days usually are the same.

In the Senate: Because the Senate often recesses rather than adjourns, the "day" often continues over several calendar days. (See Recess.)

Legislative History: The trail that's left as a newly introduced bill follows the path toward becoming a law. It includes such material as the original measure and its amendments, the committee report, the conference report, and references to it in the *Congressional Record*. A law's legislative history is used to determine what Congress had in mind; it's especially helpful to agencies that must operate under that law.

Library of Congress: It was established in 1800 with five thousand dollars "for the purchase of such books as may be necessary for the use of Congress." Now, funded mainly by Congress, it's the country's national library. (See Congressional Research Service.)

Line-Item Veto: Power given to the president to veto specific parts of a spending bill without striking down the entire legislation.

Live Pair: See Pairing of Members.

Live Quorum Call: A request that members come to the chamber. It's used to summon members when important business is about to be taken up.

Lobby: A group exercising its constitutional right to petition the government. It seeks to influence members in order to further its own cause. Professional lobbies and lobbyists are regulated by law.

The president of the United States may sometimes

lobby the Congress in order to assure passage of legislation he favors. And you and I individually may lobby our representatives and senators.

Logrolling: A bargaining strategy in which members trade votes in order to ensure passage of a measure that's of special interest to them. (See Rider.)

M.

Majority Leader: The floor leader and chief strategist of the party holding more than half the seats in the chamber. The majority leaders of both House and Senate help plan daily, weekly, and annual legislative agendas; confer with the president about administration proposals; lobby colleagues for and against measures; and work to advance the program of the party. Their salaries are higher than other members', and a car and driver and a separate leadership office go along with the office. (See Minority Leader.)

In the House: The Speaker's principal deputy, the majority leader is elected every two years by secret ballot of the party caucus.

In the Senate: He is elected at the start of each new Congress by a majority vote of the senators in his party. Because a good deal of the Senate's work is accomplished by unanimous consent, the majority leader must be in almost continuous consultation with the minority leader.

Majority Whip: The assistant majority leader, he's elected by his party's caucus. The whip helps marshal majority forces in support of party strategy, encourages party discipline, and makes sure members show up for votes and quorum calls. He also canvasses members on pending issues in order to help the floor leader gauge who and how many are for and who and how many are against a proposed piece of legislation. (See Minority Whip.)

Manager: The name given to a member of a conference committee.
In the House: It's also the name given to members appointed by the Speaker or elected by the House to carry articles of impeachment to the Senate.

Mandatory Spending: Spending (budget authority and outlays) controlled by laws other than annual appropriations acts. They cover such entitlements as Social Security and Medicare.

Markup: The process by which a bill's final language is determined and written down. When hearings are concluded, the committee or subcommittee processing the bill does this job. In accord with the rules of both House and Senate, committee markup sessions must be open to the public. (See Clean Bill.)

Memorial: A request by a citizens' group or organization for congressional opposition to a particular piece of legislation or to a government practice. (A request for support is referred to as a petition.) All communications from a state legislature, whether for or against a piece of legislation, take the form of a memorial. Memorials are usually referred to the appropriate committees for handling.
In the Senate: The memorial is put aside if the matter it deals with has already been reported out of committee. During the amendment process of the appropriate bill, the memorial can be called up for consideration.

Messages: The president, the Senate, and the House frequently exchange material—for example, letters, conference reports, and enrolled bills—all of which is referred to as messages. Such material is said to be "messaged" to the chamber receiving it. Chamber rules prescribe how and by whom messages shall be conveyed.

In the House: If the House is in the Committee of the Whole when a message arrives, it dissolves itself by rising and the Speaker resumes the chair in order to receive the message.

Minority Leader: Titular head of the loyal opposition and floor leader of the party holding fewer than half the seats in each chamber. His duties are much the same as those of the majority leader, and he receives the same perks. (See Majority Leader.)

In the Senate: Because a good deal of the Senate's work is accomplished by unanimous consent, the minority leader must be in almost continuous consultation with the majority leader.

Minority Whip: Assistant to the minority leader, he's elected by his party's caucus. His role is similar to that of the majority whip. (See Majority Whip.)

Modified Rule: Ordered by the House Rules Committee, this is one type of resolution that sets out how a bill will be handled on the House floor. It allows amendments to some parts of a bill but not to others.

Morning Business: The housekeeping matters taken up by the House and Senate during the so-called morning hour.

In the Senate: With unanimous consent, morning business may be returned to throughout the day.

Morning Hour: The time at the start of each legislative day when morning business is taken up.

In the House: Each member is allowed to give a one-minute speech during this time.

In the Senate: Officially the first two hours of the legislative day, it's often held following a recess as well. It's a time when routine business is taken up: receiving of messages; committee reports; presentation of petitions and memorials. Bills and resolutions may also be introduced and briefly explained.

During the first hour no motion to consider a bill on the Calendar of Business is in order, except by unanimous consent. However, during the second hour such motions may be made although no debate is allowed. (See Motion to Consider.)

Motion: A request by a member for any of a variety of parliamentary actions. The order in which motions can be taken up and whether they are debatable is set forth in the House and Senate rules.

Motion to Consider: A request to call up a bill.

In the Senate: A motion to proceed to consider. It's a way to bring a measure to the floor when unanimous consent to do so can't be obtained. Brought during the morning hour, it's not debatable, but brought at any other time, it is debatable and so may be subject to a filibuster. Its adoption is by majority vote.

Motion to Recommit: See Recommittal Motions.

Motion to Reconsider: See Reconsider a Vote.

Multiple Referral: The practice of assigning a bill to more than one committee. A bill may be assigned: (1) to two or more committees jointly; (2) sequentially, first to one and then to another committee; (3) or to a number of different committees, giving each jurisdiction over a specific part of the measure.

In the House: The parliamentarian, acting for the Speaker, decides which committees get which bills. A committee of primary jurisdiction must be named.

In the Senate: Action by the joint leadership or unanimous consent is needed before a measure may be jointly or sequentially referred.

Must Pass Bill: A vitally important measure that Congress must enact, such as annual money bills to fund government operations. Because of their must-pass quality, such bills attract riders.

N.

National Archives and Records Administration (NARA): The place where official records of the House and Senate concerning pieces of legislation, nominations, and treaties are stored. The material is open for research purposes in accord with the rules of the House and Senate.

Nominations: The Constitution says that the president shall nominate and by, and with the advice and consent of the Senate, shall appoint ambassadors, other public ministers and consuls, justices of the Supreme Court, and all other officers of the United States. The Senate treats nominations as it does any other measure: through the committee and subcommittee process. The full committee may report a nomination favorably, unfavorably, or without recommendation, or it may take no action at all. A majority vote of the Senate is needed for final passage.

Nominations are called up on the Executive Calendar. If they haven't been acted upon by the end of a session, they die and must be resubmitted by the president. A recess of more than thirty days also requires that they be returned to the president. (See Senatorial Courtesy.)

Nongermane Amendment: An amendment that has nothing to do with the subject of a bill. If a bill's about baseball and the amendment's about football, it's nongermane. (See Germane; Rider.)
In the Senate: Rules allow nongermane amendments in all but a few specific circumstances.

Notice Quorum Call: A special quorum call used in the Committee of the Whole. The chair announces in advance that if during a quorum call he decides that a quorum is present, he may declare that a quorum is constituted, stop the call in midstream, and get on with the committee's business.

O.

Oath of Office: At the beginning of each new term all members swear allegiance to the Constitution and that they will carry out the duties of their office. In the House the oath is usually administered by the Speaker, and in the Senate by the vice president.

Objectors: Members assigned the task of seeing that measures warranting full debate or that are unfavorable to their party's cause are not pushed through the chamber without their party's knowledge and consent.
In the House: 1. Six members (three from the majority and three from the minority) screen private bills before they are called up on the Private Calendar. They will

object to any measure they think does not meet that calendar's requirements.

2. Six members (three from the majority and three from the minority) who screen bills on the Consent Calendar. They will object to any measure they think important enough or with enough opposition to warrant full debate.

In the Senate: The Democratic and Republican policy committees screen private bills reported by the Committee of the Judiciary. They make sure that objections will be raised to any measure that is at odds with their respective parties' objectives.

Off-Budget Entities: Agencies such as the Postal Service, whose budgets are not included in the spending limits established by the budget act.

Office of Management and Budget (OMB): A support agency to the president. OMB acts as a central clearinghouse, coordinating and sifting through the recommendations made to the president by party platforms, Congress, pressure groups, etc. It helps the president develop a legislative program by deciding how and where federal funds should be spent.

Office of the Floor Assistants: Known officially as the Speaker's Office for Legislative Floor Activities, it was set up to help the Speaker manage legislative floor activity.

Office of the General Counsel: It provides legal assistance to the House and its members and committees. Legislative counsel are nonpartisan and make sure that a bill is written so that it says what its sponsors want it to say.

Omnibus Bill: A piece of legislation made up of several bills. In both chambers one objection to a particular bill is enough to eliminate it from the package. When passed, the omnibus bill reverts back to the many bills of which it's composed, and each is engrossed and sent to the other chamber as if it had been individually passed. (See Objectors.)

In the House: Omnibus bills that are made up of private bills or resolutions that have previously been objected to on a call of the Private Calendar are given preference on the third Tuesday of each month.

In the Senate: On the Calendar of Business, omnibus bills may be taken up any day after the close of the morning hour.

One-Minute Speech: An address to the House that may not exceed one minute in length but that may be on any subject. One-minute speeches are usually given at the beginning of the legislative day, when time is set aside for members to ask for unanimous consent to address the House for one minute. The Speaker may occasionally recognize a member at another time, but he does so only out of courtesy and not by rule. A call for regular order ends such speeches.

Open Rule: Ordered by the House Rules Committee, this type of resolution sets out how a bill will be handled on the House floor. It allows all germane amendments (amendments that are directly related to the bill) to be considered. A **wide-open rule** allows extended debate and amendments.

Other Body: Members of the House refer to the Senate as such. They may refer to the existence of the Senate and its functions in a general and neutral way. Such references are okay, and the term "other body" need not be used. However, in debate it's discourteous to refer to Senate action, debate, or votes on the same subject being discussed in the House. Members may not read or quote from the speeches or proceedings of the Senate.

Override a Veto: See Veto.

Oversight Committee: A committee or subcommittee of the House or Senate that keeps tabs on how the executive branch, through its agencies, is administering the laws Congress has passed.

PAC: Acronym for "political action committee." PACs supply campaign funds to candidates with whom they are compatible. They represent such groups as labor unions, corporations, and trade and professional societies. They are regulated by campaign financing laws.

Pairing of Members: The way for a member expecting to be absent when a roll call vote is taken, to go on record as having voted. Pairs do not appear in the vote totals, but their names and stands (if known) are printed in the *Congressional Record*.

In a **regular pair** an absent member asks to be paired with another who is absent but holds an opposing view. In a **general pair** both members are absent, but neither indicates his view. In a **live pair** one member may be absent and the other present, but they are of opposing views and the member who is present refrains from casting his vote. On questions requiring a two-thirds majority, members are paired two for and one against. *In the House:* General pairs are the most often used. The clerk announces all pairs just before the chair announces the result of a vote.

Papers: The original bill or resolution, its amendments as well as its conference report. The question of which chamber has custody of the papers is sometimes vital, as only the chamber having them in its possession may call a conference or take action on a conference report. (See Second Chamber.)

Parliamentary Inquiry: A request for information or an explanation of a question of parliamentary procedure.

Party Committees: In both the House and Senate, Republicans and Democrats have party committees. In general, **steering committees** see to committee assignments, and **policy committees** advise on legislation and party action. **Campaign committees** help raise money for and give support to candidates of their choice.

Perfecting Amendment: An amendment that does nothing to the real meaning of a measure, but rather makes the text itself correct. This must be done before the question to delete or add the material as a whole is put.

Permanent Appropriation: Budget authority that becomes available as the result of previously passed legislation; it doesn't require current action by Congress. It is considered current if provided in the current session of Congress and permanent if provided in prior sessions.

Personal Staff: Aides to members. Personal staffs may handle constituent services, correspondence, and public relations and give clerical, legal, and legislative help. In general, **administrative assistants** (AAs) run the office, and **legislative assistants** (LAs) work on and keep the member up to scratch on legislation. (See Committee Staff.)

In the House: House rules control how many aides each member may have in Washington and in his district offices, as well as their pay scale.

In the Senate: Rules set the amount of money a member is given for staff according to the size of the state he represents. A member may hire as many aides as he wishes as long as he keeps within his allowance.

Petition: A request by a citizens' group or organization for support on a particular piece of legislation or for favorable consideration of a matter not yet on the congressional agenda. In both chambers petitions are sent to the appropriate committees for disposition. (See Memorial.)

Pocket Veto: A way for the president to kill a piece of legislation by taking no action. If the president doesn't sign a bill within the ten days allowed, and if during those ten days Congress adjourns without setting a time for reconvening, the bill doesn't become law even though he has exercised no formal veto.

Point of Order: An objection raised when it's thought the chamber is violating its own rules. The objecting member cites the rule he believes violated and explains the objection. Another member may speak against the objection. With the help of the parliamentarian the chair rules on the objection, either sustaining or rejecting it. Because the discussion is permanently recorded as a precedent, members may not revise or extend their remarks on a point of order. (See Appeal; Precedents.)

In the Senate: After cloture has been invoked, points of order are no longer debatable. Points of order concerning germaneness are often brought against amendments to general appropriation bills. Without debate the Senate then votes on the question.

Political Action Committee: See PAC.

Pork Barrel: Legislation that calls for a government project or appropriation that opens the door for patronage and brings federal funds to a member's district or state. It's usually done with an eye to reelection. As an example, Senator X may push for a federal dam and Representative Y for a military base. (See Christmas Tree Bill.)

Preamble: An introduction to a measure that states the measure's intent; its clauses follow the word "Whereas" and precede the enacting or resolving clause. A preamble can be amended only after the measure it accompanies has been passed or adopted. A separate vote is taken on the preamble whether or not it has been amended.

Precedents: These are past decisions that have become guides on which to base future behavior. A precedent is set each time a chamber interprets its rules. If they're set by a vote, they carry great weight. A precedent can be reversed by a different majority voting at a different time. What you have then is a new precedent.

Previous Question Motion:
In the House: A device used to cut off debate and force a vote on the measure being considered. Until the pre-

vious question is moved and passed, a bill and its amendments are subject to further debate and amendment.

Private Bill: A proposed law that deals with matters touching upon an individual—for example, an individual's immigration or naturalization case. (See Bill; Private Calendar; Private Law.)

Private Calendar: A Calendar of the Committee of the Whole House that contains private bills—for example, immigration requests or claims against the government. Most bills on this calendar are passed without debate. If two or more members do object, the bill is sent back to committee. This calendar is called on the first and third Tuesdays of each month. A two-thirds vote is needed to dispense with the calling of the calendar on the first Tuesday. (See Omnibus Bill.)

Private Law: A private bill, one dealing with matters concerning a person, that has been enacted into law becomes a private law.

Privilege: The right to immediate consideration of matters affecting the rights, safety, dignity, and integrity of the chamber or its members. Also the relative priority of motions and other actions in the chamber. For the rights of members collectively, see Questions of Privilege. For the rights of individual members, see Questions of Personal Privilege. For the relative priority of legislative business, see Privileged Questions.

Privileged Questions: The relative priority of legislative business—the order in which bills, motions, etc. may be taken up in the chamber. All questions are not equal. For example, a motion to recommit is less privileged than a motion to table, but a motion to adjourn, considered of the highest privilege, would take precedence and be voted upon before either of the two others.

Pro Forma Amendment: An amendment made as a matter of form; it makes no change in a measure's language or substance.
In the House: One example of such an amendment is a member's asking to "strike the last words." It's used for purposes of debate or explanation, and no actual amendment is contemplated. No words are actually cut out, but because the member has requested the amendment, he's given five minutes in which to speak.

Pro Forma Session: Neither the House nor Senate can adjourn for more than three days without asking the other's permission. To get around this, a pro forma session is held. That's when a member brings the chamber to order and then immediately adjourns it. The process may take only a minute or two, but it counts as a day's session.

Proxy Voting: Authorizing another member to cast one's vote in one's absence. It's not allowed on either the House or Senate floor or in committees of the House. (See Pairing of Members.)
In the Senate: Proxies may be voted in committees only if the absent member has been informed of the matter on which he is being recorded and has requested he be recorded.

Public Bill: A proposed law dealing with general matters. (See Bill; Public Law.)

Public Debt: Cumulative amounts borrowed by the Treasury Department or the Federal Financing Bank from the public or from another fund or account. It's subject to a statutory limit.

Public Law: A public bill, a bill dealing with general matters, that has been enacted into law becomes a public law.

2.

Question of Consideration: When a motion or proposition has been made, the question "Will the House now consider it?" may be put upon the demand of a member. It's one way the House protects itself from business it doesn't want to take up.

Questions of Personal Privilege: Questions of privilege that concern individual members. They are decided before almost all other proceedings.

Questions of Privilege: Matters concerning the rights, safety, dignity, and integrity of proceedings of the chamber itself.

Quorum: The number of members who must be present in order that business can be conducted. In fact, unless a member suggests otherwise, a quorum is assumed to be present no matter how many are in attendance.
In the House: Two hundred and eighteen members in the House and one hundred in the Committee of the Whole make up a quorum. A quorum call is sometimes used as a way to get members to come to the floor of the House. It is usually taken by electronic device with

members simply voting "present." (See Notice Quorum Call.)

In the Senate: Fifty-one members constitute a quorum. The Senate has frequent quorum calls, which usually are used to fill gaps between legislative matters. They are rarely completed, being stopped in midstream by unanimous consent. (See Live Quorum Call.)

$\mathscr{R}$

Ranking Member: The member of the majority party on a standing committee, who is next in seniority to the chair.

Ranking Minority Member: The chief member of the minority party on a standing committee, he's usually the person with the most seniority, the one who's been there longest. The ranking minority member appoints and supervises the committee's minority staff and in general looks out for his party's interest.

Reading of the Bill: Historically a bill was read three times before it was passed. Now a reading of its title may be all that's needed.

In the House: A bill is considered to have had its first reading when it's introduced and printed, by title, in the *Congressional Record*; its second, when floor considerations begin (if there is an actual reading, it's most likely to occur now); its third, usually by title, when action has been completed on amendments.

In the Senate: The rules state that a bill or joint resolution must be read three times on three different legislative days. If, however, there's no objection, after it's been introduced and before it's referred to committee, it's read twice by title. When all consideration of a measure is concluded, a motion comes on engrossment and a third reading. This reading is usually only by title, but a full reading may be demanded.

Reapportionment: The number of House members is set by statute at 435. House seats are reallocated every ten years on the basis of the population figures supplied by the new census. If a state's population increases, so may the number of its representatives; if its population decreases, so may the number of its representatives. Illinois's loss may be Indiana's gain.

Recess: To suspend business at the end of the day's session. By doing this instead of adjourning, when it next meets, the House or Senate may resume its business at the point it left off. The House most often adjourns while the Senate most often recesses.

Recommittal Motions: There are two kinds of recommittal motions that may be made after deliberation on a bill: 1. a **simple motion to recommit,** to return the bill to the committee that reported it. If this passes, it kills the bill; 2. **a motion to recommit with instructions**, which asks the committee to report the bill back with amendments. If this motion is adopted, the bill isn't actually sent to the committee, but the amendments automatically become part of the bill. Motions to recommit are seldom used in the Senate.

Reconciliation Bill: A bill that makes changes in legislation already enacted or enrolled, to assure that the expenditures laid down in the concurrent budget resolution will be met. Like all bills, it must be passed by both chambers and signed by the president. (See Reconciliation Resolution.)

Reconciliation Process: It's how Congress changes existing laws to conform tax and spending levels to those set in a budget resolution.

Reconciliation Resolution: A measure, passed by both chambers that changes unfinished legislation to assure that the targets set for both spending and revenues will be met. Like all resolutions, it must be passed by both chambers, but it doesn't need approval of the president. (See Concurrent Budget Resolution; Reconciliation Bill.)

Reconsider a Vote: In both House and Senate a motion to reconsider suspends action on a measure just voted upon. The motion is usually made immediately after a measure has been passed and is almost always tabled, thus shutting off any future reconsideration except by unanimous consent. If the motion to reconsider is agreed to, another vote may be taken on the measure. A majority vote is needed either to affirm the original vote or to reverse it.

In the House: The motion to reconsider can be made on the day a measure passes or on the next succeeding day the House is in session. It can be made only by a member who voted with the majority.

In the Senate: The motion to reconsider can be made on the same day or on either of the next two days of actual session after a measure's passage. It can be made only by a senator who either voted with the majority or did not vote at all. But if the bill passed by either a voice vote or a division vote, any member may make the motion.

Recorded Vote: A vote in which a member's individual stand is noted. In the full House or in the Senate, see Roll Call Vote. In the Committee of the Whole, see Teller/Recorded Teller Vote.

Regular Meeting Day: In the Senate, Rule XXVI requires that each standing committee (with the exception of the Committee on Appropriations) designate at least one day a month on which it will meet to transact business. Additional meetings may be called by the chair or by demand of a majority of a committee's members.

Regular Order: The order in which business is scheduled to be taken up during the day's session.
In the Senate: Members may call for regular order when they think a vote is concluded and wish the results to be announced.

Regular Pair: See Pairing of Members.

Report:
   1. A committee-prepared description of the purposes and provisions of a piece of legislation. Most reports ask for a bill's passage. If a report isn't unanimous, the dissenting committee members may file a minority report. Reports become an important part of a measure's legislative history, helping show what Congress had in mind at the time. House and Senate reports are designated "H. Rept." and "S. Rept." followed by a number.
In the House: For each roll call vote in a full committee, it's required that each committee report show the number of votes cast for or against and the names of those voting for or against each amendment to the measure and the motion to report it to the House.
   2. To announce. A subcommittee reports a bill to a

full committee, which in turn may report the bill to the House or Senate—that is, make the chamber aware of the committee's findings and recommendations regarding a bill.

Reprimand: The House or Senate may reprimand a member it believes is guilty of wrongdoing. This is the least of the disciplinary measures a chamber may take. (See Censure; Expulsion.)

Rescission: A tactic used by the president to hold back previously appropriated funds that have not yet been spent. If the House and Senate haven't approved the president's action within forty-five days, the president must release the funds. (See Deferral; Impoundment of Funds.)

Resolution: See Concurrent Resolution; Joint Resolution; Simple Resolution.

Resolution of Inquiry: The House and Senate have the right to ask the president and heads of executive departments for information, and this is the resolution that's used to do it. (See Executive Privilege.)
In the House: A committee sent such a resolution for action must report back to the House within fourteen days.

Resolution of Ratification: The way our nation confirms its willingness to enter into a treaty. It may include reservations—modifications or limitations that substantially affect one or more of the treaty's provisions—or understandings and statements that don't modify or limit the treaty's provisions but instead clarify or explain them. For passage, a resolution of ratification needs a vote of two thirds of the senators present.

Resolving Clause: The key paragraph that appears at the start of every resolution begins with the words "Be it Resolved . . ." A successful motion to strike the resolving clause kills the measure. (See Enacting Clause.)

Revenue Neutral: A measure that specifies exactly how any funds required to make it work will be raised. Such measures, sometimes also referred to as outlay neutral, may shift funds from other parts of the budget or call for additional taxes.
In the House: A three-fifths majority is needed to pass any bill that would raise either personal or corporation taxes.

Riddick's Senate Procedure: Named after Senate Parliamentarian Emeritus Floyd M. Riddick, it contains the contemporary precedents and practices of the Senate. It's updated periodically by the Senate parliamentarian.

Rider: A nongermane amendment, one that has nothing to do with the subject of a bill. When a bill is blocked in committee, the Senate may add it as a nongermane floor amendment to another bill. Nongermane amendments may sometimes be the result either of logrolling or of courtesy extended to a member who strongly favors the measure. They're sometimes approved simply because they're popular, but with full knowledge that they will be dropped in conference. (See Appropriation Riders; Christmas Tree Bill.)

Rising: 1. The act of getting to one's feet in order to be recognized by the presiding officer. "For what reason does the gentleman rise?" asks the chair.

2. The way a committee suspends its operation. It rises.

In the House: The Committee of the Whole dissolves itself—suspends its operation—by rising. When it does so, the House automatically is in session.

Roll Call Vote: A recorded method of taking the yeas and nays. Members are usually given fifteen minutes in which to vote.

In the House: It's used only in the House and not in the Committee of the Whole (see Teller/Recorded Teller Vote). It's usually taken by the electronic voting system, but the Speaker has the right to order an actual call of the roll. The Speaker may himself vote if he wishes, and he *must* vote when there's a tie.

The yeas and nays are automatically required if a member objects to holding a nonrecorded vote and a quorum is not present. The yeas and nays may also be ordered to be taken by a vote of one fifth of those present.

In the Senate: The yeas and nays are ordered by one fifth of those present with a minimum of eleven required. However, if a senator insists on a recorded vote, his request is seldom denied. A member may not vote after the presiding officer has announced the decision but may, with unanimous consent, change or withdraw his vote.

Rule: A standing order dealing with the duties of officers, order of business, voting procedures, and other matters necessary for the chamber to get on with its work. The House adopts its rules on the first day of each Congress. Because the Senate is a continuing body, its rules remain in force from one Congress to the next.

In the House: A rule is also a resolution reported by the

House Rules Committee concerning when and how a particular bill will be handled on the House floor—conditions for its debate and amendment. There are four major types of standing rules (see Closed Rule; Modified Rule; Open Rule; Waiver), as well as a special rule (see Special Resolution), that may be reported.

Rules Committee: The House Committee on Rules decides when a bill will come to the floor and draws up the rule under which the bill will be debated and amended. Usually it's the chair of the committee reporting a bill who asks for a rule from the Rules Committee. The committee debates the request in the same way any committee would consider legislation and reports it to the House. When not considered immediately, the rule is placed on the calendar. The Senate has no such committee, but see Unanimous Consent Agreement.

S.

Scorekeeping: Keeping track of congressional budget actions and comparing them with targets and ceilings set in concurrent budget resolutions, etc. Compiling and publishing such data are the jobs of the Congressional Budget Office.

Second Chamber: The name sometimes used to indicate the chamber that isn't the originator of a measure. For example, after a bill has been passed by the House, the engrossed copy is submitted to the second chamber, the Senate, for its consideration. (See Papers.)

Secret Session: Sometimes called closed session. When confidential communications are received from the president, or when the Speaker, presiding officer, or any member informs the House or Senate that he has communications that he believes ought to be kept secret, the chamber may be cleared of everyone except its members. Certain designated officers and employees who the Speaker or presiding officer thinks are necessary to the functioning of the session are allowed to stay but must sign an oath of secrecy. Transcripts of such sessions are referred to the appropriate committees for evaluation and may be printed in the *Congressional Record* with appropriate deletions and revisions.

Select or Special Committee: This is a temporary panel that goes out of business after the two-year life of the Congress that created it. Some do become permanent committees—for example, the Senate Special Committee on Aging. Most are created only for the purpose of looking into a given issue and lack authority to initiate legislation. They are set up by resolution of either chamber.

Selection of Conferees: Each chamber may name as many conferees as it wishes, and the ratio of Democrats to Republicans is generally the same as their proportion in the two chambers. Because each chamber votes as a unit, there is no advantage in numbers. Although House and Senate rules say that conferees will be chosen by the Speaker and the Senate's presiding officer, it's usually the chairs and ranking majority members of the committees reporting the legislation who do the choosing. (See Conference Committee.)

Senatorial Courtesy: By unwritten custom, a nominee isn't confirmed unless the senators from the president's party of the state in which the office is situated agree to the nomination. For example, if President Clinton, a Democrat, nominates a federal judge who will sit in the state of New York, he will seek the agreement of New York's Democratic senator, Daniel Patrick Moynihan. Another form courtesy takes (although it's not always honored) is in allowing nominations of senators or former senators to be confirmed without being first sent to committees.

Senior Senator: The senator with the most seniority, the one who's served longest, of the two representing a single state. (See Junior Senator.)

Session: Literally, "a meeting." There are annual and daily sessions. Each Congress must have at least one annual session. It's more usual, however, for there to be two sessions, the first during the year following the election and the second the year after that. A new session begins each January 3 at noon and continues until adjournment sine die—adjournment without setting a time for reconvening. Sessions usually end in the fall. A daily session begins when the presiding officer first calls the chamber to order at the appointed time. It extends until the chamber adjourns after having set the time of its next meeting. (See Special Session.)

Simple Resolution: A measure that affects the rules of a single chamber or expresses its feelings. It doesn't need the approval of both chambers or of the president, and it doesn't have the force of law. In the House it's designated "H. Res." followed by a number. A special order of resolutions—rules governing the time and manner of debate as set by the House Rules Committee—also uses this designation. In the Senate resolutions are designated "S. Res." followed by a number.

Special Orders: Anything outside the regular order of business of the chamber. Members request time in advance and may talk for a predetermined amount of time on any topic they wish.

In the House: It most often refers to speeches of up to one hour that are given at the end of the legislative day. The speeches may not actually be given, but their texts are included in the *Congressional Record*. Those that are delivered are governed by special rules. For example, a member won't be recognized after midnight; recognition for speeches longer than five minutes is limited (except on Tuesday) to four hours divided equally between the majority and minority, and the first hour for each party is reserved to its respective leader or his designee. (See Special Resolution.)

In the Senate: It most often refers to speeches of up to five minutes that are given before morning business is taken up. Any subject may, by a vote of two thirds of those present, be made a special order of business for consideration at a specified time.

Special Resolution: The House Rules Committee may decide to provide a special resolution or special order, one that provides for a bill's immediate consideration by the House. This rule must be passed by a two-thirds vote of the House before the bill can be brought to the floor.

Special Session: A meeting of Congress convened by the president. The Constitution gives him the power to do it. It's called after Congress, having completed its regular session, has already adjourned without setting a time for reconvening.

Sponsor: The member who's the author of a bill, resolution, or amendment and introduces it to the chamber. There is no limit to the number of cosponsors a public bill may have.

In the House: Members may ask unanimous consent that their names be added or deleted as sponsors up to the day the bill is reported from committee.

In the Senate: There is one prime sponsor of a measure, and his name appears on a reported bill or resolution and the printed report accompanying it. Cosponsors are listed when a measure is first introduced, and others may be added by unanimous consent at the measure's next printing.

Staff: See Committee Staff; Personal Staff.

Standing Committee: A permanent committee created by either public law or amendment to the House or Senate rules. Standing committees continue from Congress to Congress and are seldom eliminated or created. Almost all measures are referred to the appropriate committees and gain their approval before proceeding to the House or Senate floor. Ultimately it's the committees, selecting among the many measures introduced in each Congress, that decide which measures will reach a chamber's floor.

In the House: In a rare move the 104th Congress knocked out three standing committees and twenty-five subcommittees.

Standing Order: A rule that automatically continues from one Congress to the next.

Standing Vote: See Division Vote.

Statutory Limit on the Public Debt: The maximum amount, established by law, of public debt that can be outstanding. The limit covers virtually all debt incurred by the federal government, including borrowing from trust funds, but excludes some debt incurred by agencies.

Subcommittee: A division of a committee. Subcommittees hold hearings, mark up the bill, and then report it back to their full committees for further action.

In the House: House rules say that each committee shall have no more than five subcommittees. There are some exceptions: The Committee on Appropriations can have no more than thirteen; Government Reform and Oversight, no more than seven; and Transportation and Infrastructure, no more than six. Committee chairs send most bills on to the appropriate subcommittees, which in turn decide which bills they want to consider and which to ignore. Beginning with the 104th Congress, a subcommittee chair can't serve for more than three consecutive Congresses.

In the Senate: The number of subcommittees that any full committee may have is limited by the rule that no senator may chair more than one subcommittee of any full committee. What this rule does is limit the number of subcommittees to the number of majority-party members on the full committee.

Subpoena Power: Congress can subpoena—order— someone to appear before a committee or subcommittee to give sworn testimony. A witness who refuses to answer the subpoena or give testimony may be found in contempt and sent to prison. (See Executive Privilege.)

Substitute: A motion, an amendment, or an entire bill introduced in place of one that's pending. When passed, it kills the original measure and takes its place. A substitute may be amended. (See Amendment in the Nature of a Substitute.)

Supplemental Appropriation: An act allocating funds in addition to those in the thirteen regular annual appropriation acts. In a case where the need for funds is too urgent to wait until the passage of the next regular appropriation bill, the supplemental appropriation fills the gap between an agency's regular appropriation and the amount thought needed for its operation for the full fiscal year.

Supplemental, Minority, and Additional Views: When a Senate committee, other than the Appropriations Committee, reports a measure, committee members have three days to file statements giving their views on the measure. Their views will then be included in the committee's written report.

Suspension of the Rules:
In the House: Meant to be a time-saving way to pass noncontroversial bills. Motions to suspend are heard on each Monday and Tuesday and during the final six days of a session.

A member arranges with the Speaker in advance to be recognized in order to make a motion to suspend the rules and pass a particular bill or resolution. If printed copies of the proposed measure are available for one legislative day, no second to the motion is needed; if not, the motion must be seconded by a majority of those present and by a teller vote if requested. Debate is limited to forty minutes, and no amendments are allowed. The motion must be agreed to by two thirds of the members voting, and a quorum must be present. If the motion is not carried, the matter may be considered later under regular procedures.

The Speaker may put off final votes on suspension bills until all have been debated. They may be called up on the following day and voted upon one after the other, without interruption. He may decide to shorten the voting time to five minutes on each bill.

In the Senate: No motion to suspend is in order except on one day's notice in writing, specifying precisely the rule or part proposed to be suspended. However, with few exceptions any rule may be suspended by unanimous consent.

T.

Table: When a motion that a matter be laid upon the table is made and passed, the matter is removed from consideration. Tabling is one way to make a matter disappear without debate since neither chamber permits debate on such a motion. Pending motions connected to a tabled bill are also tabled, and when a proposed amendment goes on the table, the pending bill goes with it.

In the Senate: Another, more flexible motion, one to lie on the table, is sometimes used. Such a motion suspends action on a measure but allows it to be brought up at a later time.

Tax Expenditure: A decrease in the taxes of a particular group—for example, homeowners or oil and gas producers. It's a form of backdoor spending because neither authorizing nor appropriation committees have any say over how much is spent.

Technical Amendment: An amendment that relates to a very limited and specific matter—for example, changes in grammar, or corrections of arithmetic, or in indexing. It makes sure that $2 + 2 = 3\ 4$.

Teller/Recorded Teller Vote:
In the House: A recorded vote taken in the Committee of the Whole when demanded by one quarter of a quorum (twenty-five members).

Originally the chair appointed two tellers from opposing sides of an issue. Members passed between them, walking up the center aisle from the well toward the main doors of the chamber. In this way first the yeas and then the nays were counted. Later teller votes became recorded, requiring that members write their names on red (nay) or green (yea) cards and hand them to the tellers. When the electronic voting system was instituted, the recorded teller vote became known simply as a recorded vote, the equivalent of the roll call vote taken in the full House. Members are usually given fifteen minutes in which to vote.

Title: The name of a piece of legislation. It appears at the beginning and is a brief summary of the measure's contents—for example, "An act making appropriations for the Department of Agriculture for the Fiscal Year ending October 1, 1997, and for other purposes." It's also a portion of a bill or act—for example, "Title IX of the 1972 Education Amendments." It's usually larger than a section, which is the smallest distinct numbered subdivision.

Treaty: An agreement between the United States and another country. The Constitution says that the president must submit all treaties to the Senate for its advice and consent. Once sent to the Senate, a treaty remains there until it is either acted upon or withdrawn by the president. All treaties and the work done on them are kept secret until the Senate passes a resolution releasing them. Treaties are dealt with by the Foreign Relations Committee. If reported by the committee, a treaty is placed on the Executive Calendar. (See Resolution of Ratification.)

Trust Fund: Monies collected by the federal government and used to carry out specific programs in accord with the terms of a trust agreement or statute—for example, Social Security. Such funds are usually invested in interest-bearing government securities, and the interest earned goes into the trust fund.

U.

Unanimous Consent: Agreement by all present.
In the House: A procedure used for noncontroversial measures that may be passed by voice vote if no objection is heard.
In the Senate: The usual way that measures are brought to the chamber's floor and how a great part of the Senate's business is conducted. Its use is usually decided upon by consultation between the majority and minority leaders. It is sometimes sought as a means of ending debate on a bill or controversial amendment. (See Unanimous Consent Agreement.)

Unanimous Consent Agreement: Used by the Senate to set the rules under which a measure will be debated, it's the equivalent of a special order issued by the House Rules Committee.

Union Calendar: Officially the agenda of the Committee of the Whole House on the State of the Union. The calendar contains bills that raise or spend money. Bills are placed on the calendar in order of the date they are reported from committee. (See Calendar Wednesday.)

Upper House: The House and Senate are created equal, so there's officially no upper or lower house. However, because senators serve for longer terms, represent whole states, and may have more individual influence over what goes on, the Senate is sometimes referred to as the upper house. In the First Congress the Senate met upstairs and the House downstairs; the Senate was literally the upper house.

𝒱.

Veto: The president's method of saying no to a bill or joint resolution (other than one proposing an amendment to the Constitution). When Congress is in session, the president has ten days, excluding Sundays, in which to exercise a veto after he's received a piece of legislation; otherwise it becomes law with or without his signature. The president returns a vetoed bill to the chamber of its origin along with a message stating his objections, and the veto becomes a question of high priority. (See Pocket Veto.)

Congress can **override a veto** by a two-thirds vote of those present and voting (a quorum being present) in both chambers. Voting must be by roll call. If the vote to override succeeds in one chamber, the measure is sent on to the other. If it too passes the measure, it becomes law without the president's signature.

President Franklin Roosevelt's vetoes (both regular and pocket) totaled 635, of which 9 were overridden. Andrew Johnson didn't have as good a batting average. His vetoes totaled 29, and 15 were overridden.

Voice Vote: The standard method of voting when a matter first comes up before the House or Senate. The chair calls first for the ayes and then for the noes, and members answer in chorus. The chair then decides upon and announces the results.

In the Senate: One fifth of the senators present (but at least eleven) may demand a roll call vote before the result of a voice vote is announced.

W.

Waiver: Permission to allow a technical violation of the chamber's own rules.

In the House: A resolution issued by the Rules Committee may waive points of order against provisions of a bill or against a specific amendment that's going to be proposed.

Whips: See Majority Whip; Minority Whip.

Wide-Open Rule: See Open Rule.

Without Objection: See Unanimous Consent.

Words Taken Down: When addressing the chamber, should a member's words be offensive to another member, the House, or the Senate, he may be called to order. Upon demand of another member his words are written down at the clerk's desk and read aloud.

In the House: The chair decides whether the words are in order. If he finds them out of order, the language is erased from the verbatim material in the *Congressional Record* and the member loses the floor for the remainder of the debate.

Y.

Yea and Nay Votes: See Roll Call Vote.

Yield: To give up the floor.

In the House: The floor managers of a bill allot specific blocks of time to members for purposes of debate. A member may in turn yield to another member for a question or comment. If the amount of time isn't specified, the member yielding may reclaim his time whenever he wishes, thus effectively cutting off the member to whom he has yielded.

In the Senate: Provided he doesn't violate the rules of the Senate, a senator recognized by the presiding officer may speak on any subject for as long as he likes. He may yield temporarily for consideration of other business or to another member for a question, but he does not parcel out specific amounts of time to other members.

3

Some Frequently Heard Phrases

The House

BRINGING A MEASURE TO THE FLOOR

SPEAKER OR CHAIR: *"For what purpose does the gentle-man [woman] rise?"*
A member wishing to address the House must first stand. When recognized, he states his purpose for rising and if the Speaker or chair decides his business is in order, he's allowed to proceed.

MEMBER: *"Move to suspend the rules and pass the bill H.R. 000."*
A motion meant to save time when dealing with non-controversial bills. If the motion is agreed to, debate is limited to forty minutes and no amendments are permitted. Final votes may be carried over to another day,

when votes on these so-called suspension bills may be called one after the other, with voting time reduced to five minutes on each bill.

MEMBER: *"Ask unanimous consent to take from the Speaker's table H.R. 000 and ask for its immediate consideration."*
A request that the House take up a specified measure, one that was previously removed from consideration (tabled).

MEMBER: *"Move that the committee be discharged from further consideration of H.R. 000 and ask for its immediate consideration."*
A unanimous consent request that the House take up a noncontroversial measure.

THE COMMITTEE OF THE WHOLE

SPEAKER: *"The Speaker declares the House in the Committee of the Whole House on the State of the Union for the consideration of H.R. 000."*
With these words the Speaker can resolve the House into the Committee of the Whole without a vote of the House.

CHAIR: *"The committee shall rise."*
When the Committee of the Whole has completed action on the measures before it, it resolves itself back into the House by rising—that is, going out of existence for the time being. If the House is in the Committee of the Whole when a message from either the Senate or the president arrives, the committee rises so that the Speaker may receive the message.

DURING DEBATE

CHAIR: *"The gentleman [woman] shall suspend."*
When the House is not in order—when members are not paying attention to the person addressing the chamber—the chair asks the member having the floor to stop speaking. When order is restored, the member is allowed to proceed.

MEMBER: *"Yield for a unanimous consent request."*
A member may give part of his time to another to state briefly his position on the matter under discussion and to *"Ask unanimous consent to revise and extend my remarks at this point in the* Record.*"*

When granted, this allows a member to change or add to his remarks where they appear in the *Congressional Record.*

MEMBER: *"Reserving a point of order."*
When unsure whether another member's motion has violated the rules of the House, a member may ask for information from the member making the motion. When the maker of the motion has concluded, the member must either insist upon his point of order or withdraw it.

MEMBER: *"Reserving the right to object."*
Used when a member is unsure of the effect of a unanimous consent request. After a brief consultation he may either continue to object or withdraw his reservation.

MEMBER: *"Reserving the right to object, and I won't object."*
Here the member merely uses his right to object to obtain time to speak on the matter being consid-

ered. When he has concluded, he withdraws his reservation.

MEMBER: *"Move to strike the last word,"* or, *"Move to strike the requisite number of words."*
If no objection is heard, the member making this amendment is entitled to speak for five minutes on the matter being debated.

MEMBER: *"Yield back the balance of my time."*
So saying, the member returns the unused portion of the time he's procured to the pool of time allowed his side in the debate.

MEMBER: *"Yield myself [or another member] such time as I [he] may consume."*
Unspecified amount of time a floor manager grants for purposes of debate. When the speaker has finished, the amount of time he has used is deducted from the pool of time the floor manager controls.

MEMBER: *"Will the gentleman [lady] yield?"*
A request that the member holding the floor allow another member time to speak.

MEMBER: *"I reclaim my time,"* or, *"Reclaiming my time."*
A member who has been granted a specific amount of time during debate may in turn grant another member an unspecified portion of that time. He may, however, cut short the member to whom he's yielded and take back his time.

MEMBER: *"Strike from the* Record.*"*
If a member believes that another member's language has offended himself, another member, or the House itself, he may ask that those words be taken down for

the Speaker's consideration. If the Speaker agrees, the language is then erased from the verbatim material in the *Congressional Records*. A member whose words are held objectionable loses the floor for the remainder of the debate.

AMENDING PROCESS

MEMBER: *"Ask that the amendments be considered en bloc."*
A unanimous consent request that an amendment pertaining to more than one section of the bill or resolution be offered only once, the first time an affected section is considered.

MEMBER: *"Ask that the amendment be considered as read."*
A unanimous consent request that the clerk dispense with the reading of the amendment about to be considered.

GETTING A RECORDED VOTE

MEMBER: *"On that I ask for a division."*
After a voice vote has been taken, a member may request a nonrecorded standing vote, one in which the presiding officer actually counts the yeas and nays.

MEMBER: *"Ask for a recorded vote, pending which I make a point of order that a quorum is not present."*

CHAIR: *"The chair will count for a quorum."*
When a member asks for a recorded vote and a quorum is not present, the ayes and nays are automatically ordered to be taken. However, if a quorum is obviously not present, to save taking time for a quorum call, the member will . . .

MEMBER: *"Withdraw my request for a quorum."*

CHAIR: *"Those in favor of taking a recorded vote will rise. Evidently a sufficient number has risen. The vote will be taken by electronic device."*
If one fifth of those present in the House (not a quorum) agree, a roll call vote is ordered.

ON FINAL PASSAGE

MEMBER: *"Move the previous question."*
This motion cuts off debate and allows the matter to come to a vote.

CHAIR: *"The [bill or motion or amendment] is agreed to, and a motion to reconsider is laid upon the table."*
A pro forma motion made after a measure has passed the House. A vote in the House is not final until there has been an opportunity to reconsider it; therefore, to forestall a motion to reconsider being made at a later date, the pro forma motion is used.

CHAIR: *"The question next comes on engrossment and a third reading (by title only) of the bill."*
If carried, the bill becomes an act. However, at this time a member opposed to the bill may offer a motion to recommit to the committee that reported it.

CHAIR: *"The question is now on the final passage."*
This is a pro forma motion to reconsider and lay the motion on the table.

MEMBER: *"Recede and concur with the Senate amendments."*
A motion made when amendments in a conference report don't conform to the House's rules (they are in

technical disagreement, not in dispute). When passed, the motion allows the House to agree to either the Senate amendments or the conference modifications.

The Senate

QUORUM CALLS

SENATOR: *"Mr. President, I suggest the absence of a quorum."*

PRESIDING OFFICER: *"The clerk will call the roll."*
A simple quorum call is used to fill time between legislative matters, and a live quorum call is used to summon members to the floor when important business is pending. A quorum call can last as long as it takes to have all except excused members reach the floor or . . .

SENATOR: *"Mr. President, I ask unanimous consent that the order for the quorum call be rescinded."*

PRESIDING OFFICER: *"Without objection, so ordered."*
With the passage of this motion the quorum call is ended. The business of the chamber may once again be taken up or the member making the motion may ask for the floor and speak on any matter he wishes. He may ask for another quorum call when he has finished his statement.

AMENDMENTS

SENATOR: *"I ask unanimous consent to withdraw amendment number 000."*
A senator can withdraw his amendment at any time before action has been taken on it.

SENATOR: *"Mr. President, I send an amendment to the desk and ask for its immediate consideration."*

PRESIDING OFFICER: *"The clerk will report the amendment."*

LEGISLATIVE CLERK: *"The senator from S, Mr. Z, proposes an amendment, number 000."*
After introducing the amendment in this fashion, the legislative clerk begins to read the amendment. He is usually interrupted.

SENATOR: *"Ask unanimous consent that further reading of the amendment be dispensed with."*
The chamber almost always agrees to this request, and the reading of the amendment is stopped—often in mid-sentence.

SENATOR: *"Point of order, Mr. President. Is the amendment germane?"*
Amendments to all general appropriation bills, bills on which cloture has been invoked, concurrent budget resolutions, and measures regulated by a unanimous consent decree that insists on it must be germane—that is, pertain to the subject of the bill under discussion.

PRESIDING OFFICER: *"The chair cannot rule on germaneness but it will submit to the Senate."*
Debate isn't permitted, and the yeas and nays are taken to determine whether the amendment is or isn't germane. If it's found not to be germane, the amendment fails and cannot be included as part of the piece of legislation under consideration.

SENATOR: *"I make a point of order against the amendment as legislation upon appropriations."*

An amendment that proposes general legislation can't be made to a general appropriation bill. When the point of order is raised, the chair rules on the matter.

SENATOR: *"I will appeal the rule of the chair."*
A member may appeal to the chamber to reverse the chair's ruling. A majority vote is needed to overrule the chair.

DEBATE

PRESIDING OFFICER: *"Who yields time?"*
When the Senate is operating under a unanimous consent agreement, the majority and minority floor managers have control of the time. When a senator takes the floor without being yielded time to speak, the presiding officer will interrupt and ask who has yielded to him.

SENATOR: *"Mr. President, I yield the floor."*
Give up the floor. A senator may yield to another member for a question or he may yield so that other business may be taken up, and still retain his right to continue speaking. He may not yield time to another for a statement, however, and then reclaim it.

PRESIDING OFFICER: *"Is there further debate?"*
If no one wishes to speak on a matter, a vote may be asked for.

PRESIDING OFFICER: *"Is it the sense of the Senate that the debate shall be brought to a close?"*
One day after a motion to invoke cloture has been filed, the presiding officer, without debate, may ask for a yea and nay vote on the motion.

ROLL CALL VOTE

PRESIDING OFFICER: *"The clerk will call the roll."*
The legislative clerk calls each senator by name. After the entire roll has been called, the names of those voting aye and those voting no are announced. During the remaining time allowed for the vote (usually fifteen minutes), senators not present when their names were called come to the floor and announce their votes to the clerk, who records them on his tally sheet. When the vote is concluded, the clerk informs the presiding officer of the results.

PRESIDING OFFICER: *"Are there other senators in the chamber who wish to record their votes? If not, on this motion the yeas are 00, the nays are 00, and the motion is [is not] agreed to."*
If the motion has failed, the Senate will move on to other business. If, however, it has passed, one more step will be taken.

FINAL PASSAGE

SENATOR: *"I move to reconsider."*

SENATOR: *"Move to table."*
Immediately after a measure has passed, the motion to reconsider is made and tabled. This effectively cuts off any later debate on the matter.

4

The Legislative Day

The legislative day extends from the time the House or Senate meets after an adjournment until it next adjourns. In the House legislative days and calendar days usually are the same. Because the Senate most often recesses rather than adjourns, the legislative day may continue over several calendar days. After a recess business can be picked up at the point it was left off, but for the most part the Senate still follows the same schedule it would after an adjournment.

The House

THE HOUSE DAY
(On any day the usual order of business may be interrupted by a privileged matter.)

1. Prayer offered by the chaplain or a visiting clergyman.

2. Approval of the *Journal*. If a recorded vote is demanded on approval of the *Journal*, the Speaker may postpone it until later in the legislative day.
3. Pledge of allegiance to the flag.
4. Correction of reference of public bills. If a bill's been sent to the wrong committee, this is the time the problem is straightened out.
5. Recognition by the Speaker of members for one-minute speeches and submission of material to the *Congressional Record*.
6. Disposal of business on the Speaker's table: Messages from the president and agency heads, reports, bills, and resolutions are sent to the appropriate committees, and other miscellaneous business is dealt with.
7. Unfinished business: matters that were being considered when the House adjourned.
8. The morning hour for the consideration of bills called up by committees.
9. Legislative business in either the full House or the Committee of the Whole.
10. Recognition of members by the Speaker for special orders. These speeches may not actually be delivered, but delivered or not, the texts are inserted in the *Congressional Record*.
11. Adjournment.

THE BUSINESS OF THE DAY

The House usually follows a Monday to Thursday schedule; however, because of the press of business, it may meet on Fridays and Saturdays as well. On Monday, Tuesday, and Wednesday time is set aside for special purposes.

Monday: The House usually meets at noon.

Each and every Monday: Motions to suspend the rules and pass a bill out of the regular order may be entertained at any time.

First and third Mondays of the month: After approval of the *Journal*, the Consent Calendar is called.

Second and fourth Mondays of the month: Except during the last six days of a session, after approval of the *Journal* the Discharge Calendar is called. After the matters on the Speaker's table have been dealt with, the Committee on Government Reform and Oversight may present business relating to the District of Columbia.

Tuesday: The House usually meets at noon.

Each and every Tuesday: Motions to suspend the rules and pass a bill out of the regular order may be entertained at any time.

First Tuesday of the month: After disposal of the business on the Speaker's table, the Private Calendar is called.

Second and Fourth Tuesdays of the month: Correction day. Measures to repeal federal regulations deemed unnecessary or ill advised may be taken up under a fast-track procedure.

Third Tuesday of the month: After disposal of the business on the Speaker's table, the Private Calendar is called with preference given to omnibus bills.

Wednesday: From January to May 15 the House usually meets at 3:00 P.M.; after May 15 the House usually meets at 10:00 A.M.

Each and every Wednesday: Except during the last two weeks of a session, after the matters on the Speaker's table have been dealt with, Calendar Wednesday may be observed: The committees are called in alphabetical order so that they may bring up any of their nonprivileged bills on the House or Union Calendar.

Thursday: From January to May 15 the House usually meets at 11:00 A.M.; after May 15 the House usually meets at 10:00 A.M.

Friday: From January to May 15 the House usually meets at 11:00 A.M.; after May 15 the House usually meets at 10:00 A.M.

Saturday: From January to May 15 the House usually meets at 11:00 A.M.; after May 15 the House usually meets at 10:00 A.M.

The last six days of a session: Motions to suspend the rules and pass a bill out of the regular order may be entertained at any time.

The Senate

THE SENATE DAY

(On any day the usual order of business may be interrupted by a privileged matter or by unanimous consent of those present.)

1. Prayer. After being called to order by the president pro tempore, a prayer is offered by the chaplain or a visiting clergyman.
2. Reading and approval of the *Journal.* By unanimous consent the reading of the *Journal* is usually dispensed with, but it may be read on demand of a senator.
3. Leader time. The majority leader and the minority

leader are given time to speak (normally ten minutes each). The majority leader usually sets out the schedule of the day, but both he and the minority leader may speak on any topic they wish.

4. Special orders. Senators who have arranged in advance to do so are allowed to address the Senate for no more than five minutes on any topic they wish.

5. Routine business. Morning business is taken up during the morning hour—officially the first two hours of the legislative day, which usually begins at noon. The Senate first deals with such things as messages from the president and House, committee reports, and presentation of petitions and memorials. Bills and resolutions may also be introduced and briefly explained.

During the first hour (usually until 1:00 P.M.) no motion to consider a bill on the calendar is in order except by unanimous consent. However, during the second hour (generally between 1:00 and 2:00 P.M.) such motions may be made, although no debate is allowed.

After the first hour or when morning business has been concluded, a member can move to take up a bill out of its regular calendar order. If work on such a measure has not been concluded by the time the Senate takes up unfinished business, the bill is held over until the next morning hour.

By unanimous consent, morning business may be taken up at any time later in the day.

6. Unfinished business. After the first hour or earlier, if morning business is completed, the Senate may take up the Calendar of Business; most often, however, this is done only once or twice a month. Instead the chamber turns to the business planned for that day by the majority leader or to the matters left unfinished when it last adjourned.

A measure under discussion may be laid aside by unanimous consent, and for a time other matters may be taken up. The original matter may be returned to at a later time. This two-track system keeps the Senate from becoming bogged down in unlimited debate on controversial matters.

7. Adjournment.

5

The Rocky Road to Passage

How a Bill Becomes a Law

(For legislation originating in the House.)

Introducing a bill: A resolution or bill is introduced when it's placed in the hopper on the bill clerk's desk. Its title is then entered in the *Journal* and printed in the next day's *Congressional Record*. The bill is assigned its proper designation and number and printed.

Committee assignment: The Speaker, with help from the parliamentarian, refers the bill to the appropriate committee(s). If multiple referrals are made, a committee of primary jurisdiction is named.

Subcommittee consideration: The committee(s) assigned the bill pass it along to their subcommittee(s).

The subcommittee(s) hold hearings and mark up the bill. They may amend it or substitute an entirely new version for it, approve it as it is, or reject it before returning it to their full committee(s).

Committee consideration: The full committee may decide to hold its own hearings as part of its deliberation. When its revisions are completed, it reports the bill to the House. A committee only rarely reports a bill unfavorably; instead it simply takes no action, thereby killing the bill.

Rules Committee action: Some privileged bills go directly to the House floor, as do others that are routine or noncontroversial. The majority, however, go to the Committee on Rules, which prepares a resolution setting the conditions for debate and amendment. It then reports the rule to the House in the same manner any other committee would submit its report.

Rule considered: The resolution or rule is called up, debated, and then usually adopted.

Committee of the Whole: If the bill raises or spends money, after adoption of the rule the House resolves itself into the Committee of the Whole for its consideration. The Committee of the Whole debates and amends the bill and reports it back to the House with its recommendations: to recommit the bill (send it back to committee), to strike the enacting clause (kill the bill), or to pass the bill as amended.

House action: The House first acts on the amendments adopted in the Committee of the Whole. When they are disposed of, the question comes on the bill's engrossment—the making of the final copy of the bill and its amendments—and the bill's third reading (by title only). At this time a member may ask that the bill be recommitted—sent back to the committee that reported it—either with or without instructions. Such a motion usually fails, and a vote is then taken on final passage of the bill.

Senate action: The engrossed bill, now an act of the House, is sent to the Senate, where the parliamentarian assigns it to the appropriate committee(s). The full committee(s) refer the matter to the appropriate subcommittees. Subcommittees hold hearings and then report the bill back to the committee(s). Only on rare occasion will a bill bypass the committee process and be placed directly on the Calendar of Business.

Unanimous consent agreement: Once the bill is reported out of committee, the majority leader tries to arrange for an agreement with the minority leader on when it will be brought to the Senate floor and the rules under which it will be debated.

Senate floor action: When a bill is brought to the floor, the majority and minority floor managers are recognized by the presiding officer so that they may make brief opening statements. Amendments are then taken up in order (the committee amendments first) and debated and voted upon under the terms of the unanimous consent agreement.

Final passage: At the conclusion of debate there is a roll call vote on the bill's final passage. If there has been no unanimous consent agreement to set the time when debate shall end, the final vote comes whenever there are no more senators wishing to debate.

Senate amendments: If it's passed in identical form by both chambers, the bill is enrolled. The Senate may, however, amend the bill and ask that the House concur in its amendments. If the House agrees to the Senate amendments, the bill is enrolled. The House may choose to amend a Senate amendment and in turn ask its concurrence. A conference may be requested at any stage of the process.

Conference: Members, called managers, are assigned to the conference committee by their respective chambers. Although the number of managers may not be equally divided between the chambers, the majority of each delegation must be from the majority party of that chamber. The House and Senate may vote to give specific instructions to their conferees; these are only guidelines, however, and are nonbinding. If the managers can't reconcile their differences, they may return to their chambers for instruction or may simply report their failure. When they have reached agreement, they prepare a conference report.

Rules Committee action: The chamber agreeing to the request to go to conference acts first on the conference report. When new language in the bill would violate House rules or lead to a point of order being made against it, the bill may be sent to the Committee on Rules. The committee grants a rule waiving such points of order, and the measure is sent on to the full House.

Conference report consideration: After adopting the rule reported by the Committee on Rules, the House takes up the conference report. The report must be acted upon as a whole and agreed to in its entirety. If not passed in both chambers, it may be recommitted to the conference committee and no further action taken until the bill is again reported out.

Enrollment: After passage by both House and Senate, the papers are sent to the enrolling clerk of the House (the chamber originating the bill). An enrolled bill is prepared and printed on parchment. Certified by the clerk of the House and signed by both the Speaker and the president of the Senate, the bill, now an act, is sent to the president.

Presidential action: The president has ten days, excluding Sunday, to act on a measure before him. If he signs the act, it becomes a law, and if he does nothing and the ten days go by, it becomes a law. If Congress adjourns during the ten-day grace period and the president has not yet acted, the measure is automatically vetoed. If he doesn't approve of the bill, he may veto it, returning it to the chamber of origin without his signature and with a message stating his objections.

Overriding a veto: A two-thirds vote in both chambers is needed to override the president's veto. The question is put: "Shall the bill pass, the objections of the president to the contrary notwithstanding?" If the veto is overridden, the bill becomes law.

6

Reaching Out

How to Get Your Point Across

You hold the key to the system. You are important, and you *can* make a difference. Legislators need and want to know what their constituents think about issues. Here's how to get in touch with your representative and senators to let them know what's important to you.

1. HOW TO FIND OUT WHO REPRESENTS YOU IN THE HOUSE AND SENATE

There are any number of ways to get this information. It's no farther away than your telephone.

Some places and people you can call:

The information desk at your local library
Your town or village hall

The editor of your local paper
The political party headquarters of your choice
The League of Women Voters

Legislators' office numbers are in the yellow pages. And don't forget your next-door neighbor. He or she may be able to give you the information and perhaps some insight into what's happening at your local level.

2. How to find out what those who represent you are up to

The *Congressional Directory* is edited by the Joint Committee on Printing and available from the Government Printing Office. It has members' bios, committee assignments, and seniority rankings. It contains data about sessions, committees and their staffs, and much, much more. Your local library should have a copy or another book with similar information. It'll be in the reference section; look for books filed under Dewey decimal number 328.

The Congressional Quarterly Inc. (a private research organization) publishes the *Weekly Report*. It's a place to get information about members and legislation. Published annually, the *Congressional Quarterly Almanac* combines the information from the *Weekly Reports*.

C-SPAN: If you have cable TV, you probably receive C-SPAN and C-SPAN 2. They're carried on two channels, and both give gavel-to-gavel coverage, one of the Senate and one of the House. The only thing that will bring you closer to the action is actually being there.

3. How to make contact with your representative and senators

By Mail Letters count—and are counted. If you've something to say about a matter that's being worked on, be sure to mention its number—for example, H. 12 or S. Res. 13. You may simply want to state your position on a bill or indicate that you want your representative to support or not support a measure. Whatever your message, try to keep it to a page or less. Handwritten letters are okay, but typed ones are easier to read.

Keep away from preprinted postcards and canned messages supplied by groups that are lobbying for their positions. They just don't have the impact of a freshly created piece.

If you don't know the addresses of your members of Congress, you can write to them care of the U.S. Senate, Washington, DC 20510 or the House of Representatives, Washington, DC 20515.

Salutations may read: "Dear Senator X" or simply "Dear Senator." In letters to representatives choose among: "Dear (Mr. or Ms.) Y"; "Dear Congresswoman Y" or "Dear Representative Y."

On the attention meter, form letters and petitions are down low, and a letter from someone who can remind a representative that they've once met is at the top.

By E-Mail The newest way to contact your representative or senators is through your computer. See Chapter 7 to find out how you can get a representative's or senator's E-mail address.

In Your District If you would like to meet one-on-one with your representative or senators, at home contact their district offices to set up an appointment. (Check the yellow pages for the locations and phone numbers of the district offices near you.) There is one catch, however: Schedules change frequently, and it sometimes takes a couple of tries to find a time when a member of Congress will actually be in the district.

Be on the lookout for the notices most representatives send out several times a year announcing when and where they will be available to meet with their constituents.

In Washington If you plan to go to Washington, begin by writing a letter to the representative or Senators you want to see, saying you wish to schedule a meeting.

If you have a particular issue you're interested in, call the office and ask for the legislative assistant (LA for short) who handles that issue. Speak to him about scheduling a time when you may meet with your representative. The LA will intervene on your behalf with the staff scheduler and administrative assistant (AA) or chief of staff to reserve the time.

If you have no particular issue in mind and just want to drop in for a chat, you may call and ask for the scheduler or the AA directly.

Remember you have a representative and two senators. If you have a special interest you want to talk about, be sure to see the staff member who handles it in each of the three offices.

If you can't get an appointment and have an issue you'd like to discuss, you'll have to use a little ingenuity. For example, if your representative's going to be at a hearing, go there too. Get a note to him (be sure to give your name and hometown) asking if he has a moment to meet with you. He might well take the time during a lull in the action to come out and have a chat.

Whichever route you take, it's important that you introduce yourself as a constituent. And if you're connected with a group that is lobbying the representative, be sure to mention that affiliation.

4. HOW TO ATTEND A SESSION OF THE HOUSE OR SENATE

If you're in Washington and want to know what's on the House and Senate agendas for the day, you can get a recorded floor schedule by calling:

In the House: Democratic Cloakroom 202-225-1600
                      Republican Cloakroom 202-225-2020
In the Senate: Democratic Cloakroom 202-224-8541
                      Republican Cloakroom 202-224-6888

Getting into the visitors' gallery is easy. Just call your representative's district or Washington office, and ask for a pass. Technically you're supposed to get a pass only from your own representative. However, many people get passes by going into any representative or senator's office and asking for one. Galleries are open at any hour, day or night, that the chamber is in session. During the tourist season, when the galleries are crowded, you may be allowed to linger only a very few minutes. If your representative or senator is involved in a debate on a matter of special interest to you, let him know, and he can arrange to have you seated in a special gallery.

5. HOW TO ATTEND A HEARING

To see your representative or senators at work you might want to go to either a committee or subcommittee hearing or markup session, a time when the bill's actual language is determined and set down.

Hearings and markup sessions are generally held in the morning, when neither House nor Senate is in session. It's easy to get into a committee meeting: You just go into the building, through the security and X-ray machine, and on into the committee room. The problem is finding out when hearings are scheduled and where they are being held.

The *Washington Post* prints daily schedules of committee hearings. The *Congressional Record* also gives advance notice of hearings. The Internet also carries this information (see Chapter 7).

Advocacy groups know when hearings are being held. For example, you might call the Children's Defense Fund to find out when hearings on welfare issues are scheduled. You may also be receiving action alerts or legislative alerts from advocacy groups that give you the needed information concerning hearings. But be warned, schedules constantly change.

Note too that important hearings draw a large crowd, mostly people from the media, lobbyists, and the likes of you and me. So be prepared for a long line of people all waiting for seats to become available.

6. How to become part of a committee or subcommittee hearing

Testifying at a hearing is a great opportunity to participate in lawmaking. You're speaking to people to whom, in a general sense, you can give nothing of a political nature, but you may very well affect their assessment of a measure, and that's no small achievement.

If you feel strongly about an issue before Congress and have information that you think will help committee members in their decision making, you may want to ask to testify. Note that it's easier to get on the agenda if you're a victim and want to share a personal story than if you want to testify as an expert witness.

Hearings may be held either in Washington or out in the field (they're called field hearings). Washington hearings are aimed at getting information and views from members of Congress and the executive branch of government, from citizens and industrial groups, and from experts of every sort. Field hearings usually are aimed at getting information and views from regional and local organizations and institutions and average citizens.

Call the committee and ask to be put on the witness list. For field hearings the phone number's probably on the hearing announcement. If you can't find the committee number in a book at your local library, you can call the main Capitol switchboard—202-224-3121—and ask for the committee number. Be sure to send a follow-up letter confirming your request. If you don't know a committee's address, write to: Name of Committee, United States Senate, Washington, DC 20510 or House of Representatives, Washington, DC 20515.

There are two other ways you can try to get to testify: through an advocacy group or through a member's legislative assistant. It may take a long time to sell the LA on the importance of your testifying; remember, he in turn has to sell the idea of your testifying to the committee staff.

Another way to go is to write to the committee chair (you can get his name from the *Congressional Directory*) and ask to appear before his committee. Your letter should focus on your expertise and point out the uniqueness of your views.

7. IF YOU'RE ASKED TO TESTIFY AT A HEARING

If you are asked to appear, submit a detailed summary of your testimony. Committee members like to review what you have to say before you say it. Except under special circumstances, Senate committees, other than the Committee on Appropriations, require a summary twenty-four hours in advance.

The Statement Try to keep it short and to the point. Begin by stating your name and address. If you're speaking for an organization, give its name and address instead of your own. You might begin by thanking the committee for holding the hearings. State your position clearly, and if a bill is the subject of the hearing, be sure to refer to it by number. Conclude your statement by thanking the committee for giving you the opportunity to express your views and giving a summary of your basic position.

After the Statement After your statement the questioning begins. The committee chair and the ranking minority member will get the ball rolling. The others will follow in order of seniority, alternating between Republicans and Democrats. Some more important hearings feature counsel for both sides, and they'll begin the questions.

Tip: If a question has you baffled, you can gain some time for thinking by reaching for a glass of water.

Dos and Don'ts at the Hearing

Do keep your testimony down to two or three important points; then ask for questions.

Don't let the way you dress undermine your credibility. Hearings are formal occasions so dress up, not down.

Do arrive at the hearing room about a half hour early, and find out from the committee staff where you stand on the witness list and when you're likely to testify.

Don't hold staff members to what you're told; everything will take longer than you or they think.

Do be there when your name is called; it makes things easier for the committee chair and staff and will earn you brownie points.

Don't call a member of Congress by his first name; stick to Mr. Brown or Senator Blue.

Don't get into partisan politics; talk about the issue you've come to talk about.

Don't interrupt a representative or senator's question.

Don't argue when told your time is up; when it's up, it's up.

You can use visual aids, but be sure they're mounted on stiff backing so they can be placed on an easel.

If you'd like the support of your members of Congress, send them copies of your statement along with a cover letter telling about the hearing, and don't forget to ask for their support. If you want to get the issue out to a larger audience, send copies of your statement to your local paper and radio and TV stations.

7

Surfing the Internet

A Guide to On-Line Information

Much information is available on the Internet, and more is coming on-line every day. As of this writing, here are some home pages you may want to call up.

The House of Representatives Home Page:
http://www.house.gov or try
gopher://gopher.house.gov
Click on the Home Page line that says:

<u>Who's Who and How Do I Contact Them</u> for the names, addresses, and phone numbers for members, committees, and House leadership
<u>Schedules</u> for the legislative activity of the House

The Legislative Process for information about bills and resolutions being considered in the Congress, as well as current information about what's happening on the House floor and about how individual members voted on specific measures

Organization and Operations for information on the internal organization and operation of the House

On this home page information is only a click away if you're interested in visitors' maps of Capitol Hill, educational documents concerning Congress and the legislative process, and links to government efforts to improve the government via citizen output.

The Senate Home Page:
http://www.senate.gov or try
gopher://ftp.senate.gov
Click on the Home Page line that says:

Directory of Senators (by Name)
Directory of Senators (by State)
Senators with Constituent E-Mail Addresses
Senate Leadership
About the Senate Committee System
Senate Standing Committees
Select, Special, Other, and Joint Committees

Other things you may find interesting include:

A Brief History of the Senate
The Legislative Process
A Glossary of Senate Terms

Using this home page, you can even plan your visit to the Senate, take a virtual tour of the U.S. Capitol, and check out the Senate art and photo gallery.

The U.S. Government Printing Office Home Page: http://www.access.gpo.gov

Much information is available from the GPO. You can check out the Federal Register and congressional calendars, documents and reports. The *Congressional Record* and its Index are there as well as information about public laws and the United State Code (the compilation of federal legislation).

The Library of Congress Home Page: http://www.loc.gov

The Library of Congress provides three major services: LC MARVEL, LOCIS, and THOMAS.

You can go directly to **LC MARVEL** at gopher://marvel.loc.gov

This gopher includes information on Congress, including links to the text of legislation, bill summary and status, the full text of the *Congressional Record*, and E-mail addressees for members of Congress and committees.

You can go directly to **LOCIS** at **telnet://locis. loc.gov** or **140.146.254.3** (you can access LOCIS from the Library of Congress home page or gopher; however, you'll need a telnet viewer).

LOCIS is the Library of Congress On-Line Information System. Among its treasures you'll find summaries, abstracts, chronologies, and status information for legislation since 1973 and the full text of legislation since 1993. Records for the current Congress are up-to-date within forty-eight hours.

You can go directly to **THOMAS** at
http://thomas.loc.gov
This on-line public access system of legislative and congressional information is named in honor of Thomas Jefferson. It offers among other things:

E-mail addresses for members and committees of both House and Senate
Full Text of Legislation
Full Text of the Congressional Record
Bill Summary and Status including digests and legislative history of bills and amendments
Hot Legislation, which consists of links to the full text of major bills receiving floor action in the current Congress
Constitution of the United States

US Government Information Sources Home Page:
http://irridium.nttc.edu//gov_res.html
This is the place to go if you're looking for information on the executive or judicial branch of government.

C-SPAN Home Page:
http://www.c-span.org or try **gopher://c-span.org**
Click on the Home Page line that says:

Program Events to find out today's C-SPAN and C-SPAN 2 offerings

<u>Public Affairs Hotlinks</u> for a direct connection to on-line resources for following Congress, politics, and public affairs

<u>Political Resource Center</u> for information about the congress, Supreme Court, and executive branch of government

The Big Guys

Here's how to get right to the top:

White House Home Page:
http://www.whitehouse.gov
You can click to get information about:

The <u>Executive Branch</u>
The <u>First Family</u>
White House <u>Tours</u>

The President's E-Mail Address:
President@Whitehouse.gov or **http://www. whitehouse.gov/White_House/Mail/html/1Pres.1/ html**

The Vice President's E-Mail Address:
Vice.President@Whitehouse.gov or **http://www. whitehouse.gov/White_House/Mail/html/VP_1/ html**

Appendix:
The Committees of the House and Senate

House of Representatives

(With the exception of the Intelligence Committee, all are standing committees.)

COMMITTEE ON AGRICULTURE

This is the committee to go to if you're interested in:

Agriculture generally
Forestry in general and forest reserves other than those created from the public domain
Agricultural and industrial chemistry
Agricultural colleges and experiment stations
Agricultural education extension services

Agricultural economics and research

Animal industry and diseases of animals

Dairy industry

Agricultural production and marketing and stabilization of prices of agricultural products and commodities (not including distribution outside the United States)

Commodities exchanges

Crop insurance and soil conservation

Extension of farm credit and farm security

Entomology and plant quarantine

Adulteration of seeds, insect pests, and protection of birds and animals in forest reserves

Inspection of livestock, poultry, meat products, seafood and seafood products

Human nutrition and home economics

Plant industry, soils, and agricultural engineering

Rural electrification

Rural development

Water conservation related to activities of the Department of Agriculture

SUBCOMMITTEES

Department Operations, Nutrition, and Foreign Agriculture

General Farm Commodities

Livestock, Dairy, and Poultry

Resource Conservation, Research, and Forestry

Risk Management and Specialty Crops

COMMITTEE ON APPROPRIATIONS

This is the committee to go to if you're interested in:

Appropriations of revenue for the support of the federal government

Amount of new spending authority, under the Con-

gressional Budget Act, that is to be effective for a
fiscal year
Rescissions of appropriations contained in appropriations acts
Transfers of unexpended balances

SUBCOMMITTEES

Agriculture, Rural Development, Food and Drug
Administration, and Related Agencies
Commerce, Justice, State, and Judiciary
District of Columbia
Energy and Water Development
Foreign Operations, Export Financing, and Related
Programs
Interior
Labor, Health and Human Services, and Education
Legislative Branch
Military Construction
National Security
Transportation
Treasury, Postal Service, and General Government
Veterans Affairs, Housing and Urban Development,
and Independent Agencies

COMMITTEE ON BANKING
AND FINANCIAL SERVICES

This is the committee to go to if you're interested in:

Banks and banking, including deposit insurance and
federal monetary policy
Bank capital markets activities generally
Depository institution securities activities generally,
including the activities of any affiliates, except for
functional regulation under applicable securities
laws not involving safety and soundness

Economic stabilization, defense production, renegotiation, and control of the price of commodities, rents, and services

Financial aid to commerce and industry (other than transportation)

Money and credit, including currency and the issuance of notes and redemption thereof

Gold and silver, including the coinage thereof

Valuation and revaluation of the dollar

International finance

International financial and monetary organizations

Public and private housing

Urban development

SUBCOMMITTEES

Capital Markets, Securities, and Government-Sponsored Enterprises

Domestic and International Monetary Policy

Financial Institutions and Consumer Credit

General Oversight and Investigations

Housing and Community Opportunity

COMMITTEE ON THE BUDGET

This is the committee to go to if you're interested in:

Measures relating to the congressional budget process generally

Concurrent budget resolutions

Measures relating to the establishment, extension, and enforcement of special controls over the federal budget

Congressional Budget Office

COMMITTEE ON COMMERCE

This is the committee to go to if you're interested in:

Interstate and foreign commerce generally
Biomedical research and development
Consumer affairs and consumer protection
Health and health facilities, except health care supported by payroll deductions
Interstate energy compacts
Measures relating to the exploration, production, storage, supply, marketing, pricing, and regulation of energy resources, including all fossil fuels, solar energy, and other unconventional or renewable energy resources
Energy information generally
Conservation of energy resources
Measures relating to (1) the generation and marketing of power (except by federally chartered or federal regional power marketing authorities), (2) the reliability and interstate transmission of, and rate making for all power, and (3) the siting of generation facilities, except the installation of interconnections between government water power projects
Measures relating to general management of the Department of Energy and to the management of all functions of the Federal Energy Regulatory Commission
National energy policy generally
Public health and quarantine
Regulation of the domestic nuclear energy industry, including regulation of research and development reactors and nuclear regulatory research
Regulation of interstate and foreign communications

Securities and exchanges

Travel and tourism

Nuclear and other energy and nonmilitary nuclear
energy and research and development, including
the disposal of nuclear waste

SUBCOMMITTEES

Commerce, Trade, and Hazardous Materials

Energy and Power

Health and Environment

Oversight and Investigations

Telecommunications and Finance

COMMITTEE ON ECONOMIC AND EDUCATIONAL OPPORTUNITIES

This is the committee to go to if you're interested in:

Education or labor generally

Columbia Institution for the Deaf, Dumb, and Blind

Howard University

Freedmen's Hospital

Food programs for children in schools

Child labor

Convict labor and the entry of goods made by con-
victs into interstate commerce

Labor standards and statistics

Mediation and arbitration of labor disputes

Regulation or prevention of importation of foreign
laborers under contract

United States Employees' Compensation Commission

Wages and hours of labor

Vocational rehabilitation

Welfare of miners

Work incentive programs

SUBCOMMITTEES

Early Childhood, Youth, and Family

Employer-Employee Relations

Oversight and Investigations

Postsecondary Education, Training, and Life-Long
Learning

Workforce Protections

COMMITTEE ON GOVERNMENT
REFORM AND OVERSIGHT

This is the committee to go to if you're interested in:

Budget and accounting measures, generally

Overall economy, efficiency, and management of
government operations and activities, including
federal procurement

Federal paper work reduction

Federal Civil Service, including intergovernmental
per-sonnel

Status of officers and employees of the United States,
including their compensation, classification, and retirement

Measures relating to the municipal affairs of the District
of Columbia in general, other than appropriations

Holidays and celebrations

National Archives

Population and demography generally, including the
census

Postal Service generally, including the transportation
of the mails

Public information and records

Relationship of the federal government to the states
and municipalities generally

Reorganizations in the executive branch of the government

SUBCOMMITTEES

Civil Service

District of Columbia

Government Management, Information, and Technology

Human Resources and Intergovernmental Relations

National Economic Growth, Natural Resources, and Regulatory Affairs

National Security, International Affairs, and Criminal Justice

Postal Service

COMMITTEE ON HOUSE OVERSIGHT

This is the committee to go to if you're interested in:

Accounts of the House generally

Appropriations from accounts for committee salaries and expenses (except for the Committee on Appropriations), House information systems, and allowances and expenses of members, House officers and administrative offices of the House

Auditing and settling of the above accounts

Employment of persons by the House, including clerks for members and committees, and reporters of debates

Compensation, retirement, and other benefits of the members, officers, and employees of the Congress

Assignment of office space for members and committees

Disposition of useless executive papers

Federal elections generally

Matters relating to the election of the president, vice president or members of Congress

Contested elections

Corrupt practices

Credentials and qualifications

Raising, reporting, and the use of campaign contribu-
tions for candidates for the office of representative
in the House of Representatives, of delegates, and
of the resident commissioner to the United States
from Puerto Rico

Library of Congress and the House Library, the
Smithsonian Institution and the incorporation of
similar institutions, and the Botanic Gardens, except for measures relating to the construction,
maintenance, and care of the buildings and grounds

Statuary and pictures

Acceptance or purchase of works of art for the
Capitol

Purchase of books and manuscripts

Franking Commission

Printing and correction of the *Congressional Record*

Services to the House, including the House restaurant, parking facilities, and administration of the
House office buildings and of the House wing of
the Capitol

Travel of House members

SUBCOMMITTEES: none

PERMANENT SELECT COMMITTEE
ON INTELLIGENCE

This is the committee to go to if you're interested in:

Central Intelligence Agency and its director and the
National Foreign Intelligence Program

Intelligence and intelligence-related activities of all
other departments and agencies of the government

Organization or reorganization of any department or
agency of the government to the extent that it re-

lates to a function or activity involving intelligence or intelligence-related activities

Authorizations for appropriations to the above mentioned as well as to any department, agency, or subdivision, or program that is a successor to them

SUBCOMMITTEES

Human Intelligence, Analysis, and Counterintelligence

Technical and Tactical Intelligence

COMMITTEE ON
INTERNATIONAL RELATIONS

This is the committee to go to if you're interested in:

Relations of the United States with foreign nations generally

Acquisition of land and buildings for embassies and legations in foreign countries

Establishment of boundary lines between the United States and foreign nations

Export controls, including nonproliferation of nuclear technology and nuclear hardware

Foreign loans

International commodity agreements (other than those involving sugar), including all agreements for cooperation in the export of nuclear technology and nuclear hardware

International conferences and congresses

International education

Intervention abroad and declarations of war

Measures relating to the diplomatic service

Measures to foster commercial intercourse with foreign nations and to safeguard American business interests abroad

Measures relating to international economic policy

Neutrality
Protection of American citizens abroad and expatriation
American National Red Cross
Trading with the enemy
United Nations organizations

Subcommittees

Africa
Asia and the Pacific
International Economic Policy and Trade
International Operations and Human Rights
Western Hemisphere

COMMITTEE ON THE JUDICIARY

This is the committee to go to if you're interested in:

Judiciary and judicial proceedings, civil and criminal
Administrative practice and procedure
Apportionment of representatives
Meetings of Congress, attendance of members, and
    their acceptance of incompatible offices
Presidential succession
Civil liberties
Constitutional amendments
Federal courts and judges, and local courts in the ter-
    ritories and possessions
Revision and codification of the statutes of the
    United States
Immigration and naturalization
Interstate compacts generally
Claims against the United States
Bankruptcy, mutiny, espionage, and counterfeiting
National penitentiaries
Patents, the Patent Office, copyrights, and trademarks

Protection of trade and commerce against unlawful
  restraints and monopolies
State and territorial boundaries
Subversive activities affecting the internal security of
  the United States

SUBCOMMITTEES

Commercial and Administrative Law
Constitution
Courts and Intellectual Property
Crime
Immigration and Claims

COMMITTEE ON NATIONAL SECURITY

This is the committee to go to if you're interested in:

Common defense generally
International arms control and disarmament
Strategic and critical materials necessary for the com-
  mon defense
Department of Defense generally, including the de-
  partments of the Army, Navy, and Air Force
  generally
Scientific research and development in support of the
  armed services
Army, navy, and air force reservations and establish-
  ments
Ammunition depots
Forts
Arsenals
Interoceanic canals generally, including measures re-
  lating to the maintenance, operation, and adminis-
  tration of interoceanic canals
Merchant Marine Academy and state maritime
  academies

Conservation, development, and use of naval petroleum and oil shale reserves

Military applications of nuclear energy

National security aspects of merchant marine, including financial assistance for the construction and operation of vessels, the maintenance of the United States shipbuilding and ship repair industrial base, cabotage, cargo preference, and merchant marine officers and seamen as these matters relate to national security

Tactical intelligence and intelligence-related activities of the Department of Defense

Size and composition of the army, navy, Marine Corps, and air force

Selective Service

Pay, promotion, retirement, and other benefits and privileges of members of the armed forces

Education of military dependents

Soldiers' and sailors' homes

SUBCOMMITTEES

Military Installations and Facilities

Military Personnel

Military Procurement

Military Readiness

Military Research and Development

COMMITTEE ON RESOURCES

This is the committee to go to if you're interested in:

Public lands generally, including entry, easements, and grazing

Mining interests generally

Fisheries and wildlife, including research, restoration, refuges, and conservation

International fishing agreements

Forest reserves and national parks created from the public domain

Forfeiture of land grants and alien ownership, including alien ownership of mineral lands

Interstate compacts relating to apportionment of waters for irrigation purposes

Irrigation and reclamation, including water supply for reclamation projects, easements of public lands for irrigation projects, and acquisition of private lands when necessary to complete irrigation projects

Relations of the United States with the Indians and the Indian tribes

Measures relating to the care and management of Indians, including the care and allotment of Indian lands and general and special measures relating to claims that are paid out of Indian funds

Measures relating generally to the insular possessions of the United States, except those affecting revenue and appropriations

Military parks and battlefields, national cemeteries administered by the secretary of the interior, parks within the District of Columbia, and the erection of monuments to the memory of individuals

Preservation of prehistoric ruins and objects of interest on the public domain

Geological Survey

Mineral land laws, claims and entries thereunder

Mineral resources of the public lands

Mining schools and experimental stations

Marine affairs (including coastal zone management), except for measures relating to oil and other pollution of navigable waters

Oceanography

Petroleum conservation on the public lands and con-

servation of the radium supply in the United States
Trans-Alaska Oil Pipeline (except rate making)

SUBCOMMITTEES
Energy and Mineral Resources
Fisheries, Wildlife, and Oceans
National Parks, Forests, and Lands
Native American and Insular Affairs
Water and Power Resources

COMMITTEE ON RULES

This is the committee to go to if you're interested in:

Rules and joint rules (except those relating to the
    Code of Official Conduct) and order of business of
    the House
Recesses and final adjournments of Congress

SUBCOMMITTEES
Legislative and Budget Process
Rules and Organization of the House

COMMITTEE ON SCIENCE

This is the committee to go to if you're interested in:

Scientific research, development, and demonstration
    and related projects
Marine research
All energy research, development, demonstration, and
    related projects and all federally owned or operated
    nonmilitary energy laboratories
Measures relating to the commercial application of
    energy technology

Environmental research and development
Astronautical research and development, including resources, personnel, equipment, and facilities
Civil aviation research and development
National Aeronautics and Space Administration
National Space Council
Outer space, including its exploration and control
National Institute of Standards and Technology, standardization of weights and measures, and the metric system
National Science Foundation
Science scholarships
National Weather Service

SUBCOMMITTEES

Basic Research
Energy and Environment
Space and Aeronautics
Technology

COMMITTEE ON SMALL BUSINESS

This is the committee to go to if you're interested in:

Assistance to and protection of small business, including financial aid, regulatory flexibility, and paper work reduction
Participation of small-business enterprises in federal procurement and government contracts

SUBCOMMITTEES

Government Programs
Procurement, Exports, and Business Opportunities
Regulation and Paperwork
Tax and Finance

COMMITTEE ON STANDARDS OF OFFICIAL CONDUCT

This is the committee to go to if you're interested in:

Measures relating to the Code of Official Conduct

SUBCOMMITTEES: none

COMMITTEE ON TRANSPORTATION AND INFRASTRUCTURE

This is the committee to go to if you're interested in:

Transportation, including civil aviation, railroads, water transportation, transportation safety (except automobile safety), transportation infrastructure, labor and railroad retirement and unemployment (except related revenue measures)

Related transportation regulatory agencies

Coast Guard, including lifesaving service, lighthouses, lightships, ocean derelicts, and the Coast Guard Academy

Inspection of merchant marine vessels, lights and signals, lifesaving equipment, and fire protection on such vessels

Navigation and related laws, including pilotage

Registering and licensing of vessels and small boats

Rules and international arrangements to prevent collisions at sea

Public works for the benefit of navigation, including bridges and dams, other than those that are international

Measures, other than appropriations, that relate to construction or maintenance of roads and post roads

Roads and their safety

Public buildings and occupied or improved grounds of the United States generally

Measures relating to the Capitol Building and the Senate and House office buildings

Care, construction, reconstruction, and maintenance of the buildings and grounds of the Botanic Gardens, the Library of Congress, and the Smithsonian Institution

Purchase of sites and construction of post offices, customshouses, federal courthouse, and government buildings within the District of Columbia

Oil and other pollution of navigable waters

Federal management of emergencies and natural disasters

Flood control and improvement of rivers and harbors

Inland waterways

Waterpower

SUBCOMMITTEES

Aviation

Coast Guard and Maritime Transportation

Public Buildings and Economic Development

Railroads

Surface Transportation

Water Resources and Environment

COMMITTEE ON VETERANS' AFFAIRS

This is the committee to go to if you're interested in:

Veterans' measures generally

Cemeteries of the United States in which veterans of any war or conflict are or may be buried, whether in the United States or abroad, except cemeteries administered by the secretary of the interior

Compensation, vocational rehabilitation, and education of veterans

Life insurance issued by the government on account of service in the armed forces

Pensions of all the wars of the United States, general and special

Readjustment of servicemen to civil life

Soldiers' and sailors' civil relief

Veterans' hospitals, medical care, and treatment of veterans

SUBCOMMITTEES

Compensation, Pension, Insurance, and Memorial Affairs

Education, Training, Employment, and Housing

Hospitals and Health Care

COMMITTEE ON WAYS AND MEANS

This is the committee to go to if you're interested in:

Revenue measures generally

Revenue measures relating to the insular possessions

Deposit of public monies

Bonded debt of the United States

Reciprocal trade agreements

Customs, collection districts, and ports of entry and delivery

Transportation of dutiable goods

Tax-exempt foundations and charitable trusts

National Social Security, except (1) health care and facilities programs that are supported from general revenues as opposed to payroll deductions and (2) work-incentive programs

SUBCOMMITTEES

Health
Human Resources
Oversight
Social Security
Trade

Senate

(All are standing committees unless otherwise noted.)

COMMITTEE ON AGRICULTURE, NUTRITION, AND FORESTRY

This is the committee to go to if you're interested in:

Agricultural economics and research
Agricultural extension services and experiment stations
Agricultural production, marketing, and stabilization of prices
Agriculture and agricultural commodities
Crop insurance and soil conservation
Farm credit and farm security
Pests and pesticides
Plant industry, soils, and agricultural engineering
Animal industry and diseases
Inspection of livestock, meat, and agricultural products
Food from freshwaters
Forestry and forest reserves and wilderness areas other than those created from the public domain
Rural development, rural electrification, and watersheds
Home economics
Human nutrition

School nutrition programs
Food stamp programs

SUBCOMMITTEES
Forestry, Conservation, and Rural Revitalization
Marketing, Inspection, and Product Promotion
Production and Price Competitiveness
Research, Nutrition, and General Legislation

COMMITTEE ON APPROPRIATIONS

This is the committee to go to if you're interested in:

Appropriation of revenue for the support of the federal government
Rescission of appropriations contained in appropriation acts
New spending authority under the Congressional Budget Act of 1974

SUBCOMMITTEES
Agriculture, Rural Development, and Related Agencies
Commerce, Justice, State, and Judiciary
Defense
District of Columbia
Energy and Water Development
Foreign Operations
Interior
Labor, Health and Human Services, and Education
Legislative Branch
Military Construction
Transportation
Treasury, Postal Service, and General Government
Veterans' Administration, Housing and Urban Development, and Independent Agencies

COMMITTEE ON ARMED SERVICES

This is the committee to go to if you're interested in:

Common defense generally
Strategic and critical materials necessary for the common defense
Departments of Defense, the Army, the Navy, the Air Force generally
Aeronautical and space activities peculiar to or primarily associated with the development of weapons systems or military operations
Military research and development
National security aspects of nuclear energy
Naval petroleum reserves, except in Alaska
Maintenance and operation of the Panama Canal, including the Canal Zone
Selective Service System
Pay, promotion, retirement, and other benefits and privileges of members of the armed forces
Overseas education of civilian and military dependents

SUBCOMMITTEES
Acquisition and Technology
Airland Forces
Personnel
Readiness
Seapower
Strategic Forces

COMMITTEE ON BANKING, HOUSING, AND URBAN AFFAIRS

This is the committee to go to if you're interested in:

Banks, banking, and financial institutions
Deposit insurance

Issuance and redemption of notes
Federal monetary policy, including Federal Reserve
  System
Control of prices of commodities, rents, and ser-
  vices
Economic stabilization and defense production
Export and foreign trade promotion
Export controls
Financial aid to commerce and industry
Money and credit, including currency and coinage
Nursing home construction
Public and private housing, including veterans'
  housing
Renegotiation of government contracts
Urban development and mass transit

SUBCOMMITTEES

Financial Institutions and Regulatory Relief
Housing Opportunity and Community Development
Housing and Urban Development Oversight and
  Structure
International Finance
Securities

COMMITTEE ON THE BUDGET

This is the committee to go to if you're interested in:

Federal budget generally
Concurrent budget resolutions
Congressional Budget Office

SUBCOMMITTEES: none

COMMITTEE ON COMMERCE, SCIENCE, AND TRANSPORTATION

This is the committee to go to if you're interested in:

Interstate commerce and transportation generally
Coast Guard
Coastal zone management
Merchant marine and navigation
Marine and ocean navigation, safety, and transportation, including navigational aspects of deepwater ports
Inland waterways, except construction
Marine fisheries
Panama Canal and interoceanic canals generally
Transportation and commerce aspects of outer continental shelf lands
Nonmilitary aeronautical and space sciences
Oceans, weather, and atmospheric activities
Communications
Standards and measurement
Regulation of consumer products and services, including testing related to toxic substances other than pesticides
Regulation of interstate common carriers, including railroads, buses, trucks, vessels, pipelines, and civil aviation
Highway safety
Sports

SUBCOMMITTEES

Aviation
Communications
Consumer Affairs, Foreign Commerce, and Tourism
Oceans and Fisheries

Science, Technology, and Space
Surface Transportation and Merchant Marine

COMMITTEE ON ENERGY AND NATURAL RESOURCES

This is the committee to go to if you're interested in:

Energy policy
Energy regulation and conservation
Energy research and development
Nonmilitary development of nuclear energy
Energy-related aspects of deepwater ports
Solar energy systems
Coal production, distribution, and utilization
Mining education and research
Mining, mineral lands, mining claims, and mineral conservation
Extraction of minerals from oceans and outer continental shelf lands
Hydroelectric power, irrigation, and reclamation
Naval petroleum reserves in Alaska
Oil and gas production and distribution
National parks, recreation areas, wilderness areas, wild and scenic rivers, historic sites, military parks, and battlefields and, on the public domain, preservation of prehistoric ruins and objects of interest
Public lands and forests, including farming and grazing thereon and mineral extraction therefrom
Territorial possessions of the United States, including trusteeships

SUBCOMMITTEES
Energy Production and Regulation
Energy Research and Development

Forests and Public Land Management
Parks, Historic Preservation, and Recreation

COMMITTEE ON ENVIRONMENT AND PUBLIC WORKS

This is the committee to go to if you're interested in:

Environmental policy
Environmental research and development
Environmental effects of toxic substances other than pesticides
Air pollution
Noise pollution
Nonmilitary environmental regulation and control of nuclear energy
Environmental aspects of outer continental shelf lands
Solid waste disposal and recycling
Water pollution
Ocean dumping
Fisheries and wildlife
Flood control and improvements of rivers and harbors, including environmental aspects of deepwater ports
Public buildings and improved grounds of the United States generally, including federal buildings in the District of Columbia
Public works, bridges, and dams
Construction and maintenance of highways
Regional economic development
Water resources

SUBCOMMITTEES

Clean Air, Wetlands, Private Property, and Nuclear Safety
Drinking Water, Fisheries, and Wildlife

Superfund, Waste Control, and Risk Assessment
Transportation and Infrastructure

COMMITTEE ON FINANCE

This is the committee to go to if you're interested in:

Revenue measures and bonded debt of the United
    States generally
Deposit of public monies
Revenue measures relating to the insular possessions
Customs, collection districts, and ports of entry and
    delivery
Tariffs and import quotas
Reciprocal trade agreements
Transportation of dutiable goods
Revenue sharing generally
National Social Security
Health programs under the Social Security Act
Health programs financed by specific tax or trust fund

SUBCOMMITTEES

International Trade
Long-Term Growth, Debt, and Deficit Reduction
Medicaid and Health Care for Low-Income Families
Medicare, Long-Term Care, and Health Insurance
Social Security and Family Policy
Taxation and IRS Oversight

COMMITTEE ON FOREIGN RELATIONS

This is the committee to go to if you're interested in:

Relations of the United States with foreign nations
    generally

Treaties and executive agreements, except reciprocal
trade agreements

Boundaries of the United States

Diplomatic service

Acquisition of land and buildings for embassies and
legations in foreign countries

National security and international aspects of trusteeships of the United States

Intervention abroad and declarations of war

Protection of U.S. citizens abroad and expatriation

Foreign economic, military, technical, and humanitar-
ian assistance

International activities of the American National Red
Cross and the International Committee of the Red
Cross

International aspects of nuclear energy

International conferences and congresses

International law as it relates to foreign policy

Measures to foster foreign trade

Measures to safeguard American business interests
abroad

Foreign loans

International Monetary Fund

Oceans and international environmental and scientific
affairs as they relate to foreign policy

United Nations and its affiliated organizations

World Bank group, the regional development banks,
and other international organizations established
primarily for development assistance purposes

SUBCOMMITTEES

African Affairs

East Asian and Pacific Affairs

European Affairs

International Economic Policy, Export, and Trade
Promotion

International Operations
Near Eastern and South Asian Affairs
Western Hemisphere and Peace Corps Affairs

COMMITTEE ON GOVERNMENTAL AFFAIRS

This is the committee to go to if you're interested in:

Archives of the United States
Budget and accounting measures other than appropriations
Census and collection of statistics, including economic and social statistics
Federal civil service
Congressional organization, except for matters amending the rules or orders of the Senate
Intergovernmental relations
Government information
Municipal affairs of the District of Columbia, except for appropriations
Organization and management of U.S. nuclear export policy
Organization and reorganization of the executive branch of government
Postal Service
Status of officers and employees of the United States, including their classification, compensation, and benefits

SUBCOMMITTEES

Investigations
Post Office and Civil Service
Oversight of Government Management and the District of Columbia

COMMITTEE ON INDIAN AFFAIRS

(Although the term "select" was removed from the committee's name in 1993, it was not made a standing committee.)

This is the committee to go to if you're interested in:

Problems and opportunities of Indians, including Indian land management and trust responsibilities, education, health, special services, loan programs and claims against the United States

SUBCOMMITTEES: none

COMMITTEE ON THE JUDICIARY

This is the committee to go to if you're interested in:

Apportionment of representatives
Judicial proceedings, civil and criminal, generally
Federal courts and judges
Local courts in the territories and possessions
National penitentiaries
Bankruptcy, mutiny, espionage, and counterfeiting
Civil liberties
Constitutional amendments
Government information
Immigration and naturalization
Interstate compacts generally
Measures relating to claims against the United States
Patent Office
Patents, copyrights, and trademarks
Protection of trade and commerce against unlawful restraints and monopolies
Holidays and celebrations

Revision and codification of the statutes of the
  United States
State and territorial boundary lines

SUBCOMMITTEES
Administrative Oversight and the Courts
Antitrust, Business Rights, and Competition
Constitution, Federalism, and Property Rights
Immigration
Terrorism, Technology, and Government Information
Youth Violence

COMMITTEE ON LABOR AND HUMAN RESOURCES

This is the committee to go to if you're interested in:

Education, labor, health, and public welfare in general
Aging
Handicapped individuals
Public health
Biomedical research and development
Child labor
Convict labor and the entry of goods made by con-
  victs into interstate commerce
Railway labor and retirement
Equal employment opportunity
Labor standards and statistics
Mediation and arbitration of labor disputes
Occupational safety and health, including welfare of
  miners
Private pension plans
Regulation of foreign laborers
Wages and hours of labor
Domestic activities of the American National Red
  Cross

Arts and humanities
Student loans
Agricultural colleges
Gallaudet University
Howard University
St. Elizabeths Hospital in Washington, DC

SUBCOMMITTEES

Aging
Children and Families
Disability Policy
Education, Arts, and Humanities

COMMITTEE ON RULES
AND ADMINISTRATION

This is the committee to go to if you're interested in:

Administration of the Senate Office Buildings and
  Senate wing of the Capitol, including assignment
  of office space
Congressional organization relative to rules and pro-
  cedures and Senate rules and regulations, including
  floor and gallery rules
Corrupt practices
Credentials and qualifications of senators, contested
  elections, and acceptance of incompatible offices
Presidential succession
Federal elections generally
Government Printing Office
Printing and correction of the *Congressional Record*
Meetings of Congress and attendance of members
Payment of money out of the contingency fund of
  the Senate
Purchase of books and manuscripts and erection of
  monuments to the memory of individuals

Senate Library and statuary, art, and pictures in the
    Capitol and Senate Office Building
Services to the Senate, including the Senate restaurant
U.S. Capitol and congressional office buildings, the
    Library of Congress, the Smithsonian Institution,
    and the Botanic Gardens

SUBCOMMITTEES: none

SELECT COMMITTEE ON ETHICS

This is the committee to go to if you're interested in:

Standards and conduct of Senate members and
    employees

SUBCOMMITTEES: none

SELECT COMMITTEE ON INTELLIGENCE

This is the committee to go to if you're interested in:

Intelligence activities of the Central Intelligence
    Agency and its director
Intelligence activities of the Defense Intelligence
    Agency
Intelligence activities of the National Security Agency
Intelligence activities of other agencies and subdivi-
    sions of the Department of Defense
Intelligence activities of the Department of State
Intelligence activities of the Federal Bureau of
    Investigation

SUBCOMMITTEES: none

COMMITTEE ON SMALL BUSINESS

This is the committee to go to if you're interested in:

Small Business Administration
Problems of American small business enterprises

<small>SUBCOMMITTEES</small>: none

SPECIAL COMMITTEE ON AGING

(No proposed legislation is referred to this committee, and it does not have the power to report legislation.)
This is the committee to go to if you're interested in:

Problems and opportunities of older people generally, including their health, income, employment, housing, and care and assistance

<small>SUBCOMMITTEES</small>: none

COMMITTEE ON VETERANS' AFFAIRS

This is the committee to go to if you're interested in:

Veterans' measures generally
Compensation of veterans
Life insurance issued by the government on account of service in the armed forces
National cemeteries
Pensions
Readjustment of service men to civil life
Soldiers' and sailors' civil relief

Veterans' hospitals, medical care, and treatment of
veterans
Vocational rehabilitation and education of veterans

SUBCOMMITTEES: none

Joint Committees

JOINT ECONOMIC COMMITTEE

What the committee does:

Conducts a continuing study of matters relating to
the president's annual Economic Report
Files a report, no later than March 1 of each year,
with the Senate and House containing its findings
and recommendations on each of the main recommendations made by the president in the Economic Report
Studies means of promoting the national policy on
employment as outlined in the Employment Act of
1946

JOINT COMMITTEE OF CONGRESS ON
THE LIBRARY

What the committee does:

Considers proposals concerning the management and
expansion of the Library of Congress, the receipt
of gifts for the benefit of the Library, the development and maintenance of the Botanic Gardens, and
the placement of statues and other works of art in
the Capitol

JOINT COMMITTEE ON PRINTING

What the committee does:

Adopts measures necessary to remedy inefficiency and
    waste in the public printing, binding, and distribu-
    tion of federal government publications

Oversees arrangement and style of the *Congressional
    Record*

Provides for printing of specific data in the *Daily
    Record*

JOINT COMMITTEE ON INTERNAL
REVENUE TAXATION

What the committee does:

Investigates the operation and effects of the federal
    system of internal revenue taxation

Index